William Shakespeare's

The Taming of the Shrew

Text by
Christopher M. Garcez
(M.A., University of Michigan at Ann Arbor)
Department of English
Hostos Community College, CUNY
Bronx, New York

Illustrations by
Arnold Turovskiy

 Research & Education Association

MAXnotes® for
THE TAMING OF THE SHREW

Printed in the United States of America

Library of Congress Catalog Card Number 96-67412

International Standard Book Number 0-87891-050-6

MAXnotes® is a registered trademark of
Research & Education Association, Piscataway, New Jersey 08854

I-1

What **MAXnotes®** Will Do for You

This book is intended to help you absorb the essential contents and features of William Shakespeare's *The Taming of the Shrew* and to help you gain a thorough understanding of the work. The book has been designed to do this more quickly and effectively than any other study guide.

For best results, this **MAXnotes** book should be used as a companion to the actual work, not instead of it. The interaction between the two will greatly benefit you.

To help you in your studies, this book presents the most up-to-date interpretations of every section of the actual work, followed by questions and fully explained answers that will enable you to analyze the material critically. The questions also will help you to test your understanding of the work and will prepare you for discussions and exams.

Meaningful illustrations are included to further enhance your understanding and enjoyment of the literary work. The illustrations are designed to place you into the mood and spirit of the work's settings.

The **MAXnotes** also include summaries, character lists, explanations of plot, and section-by-section analyses. A biography of the author and discussion of the work's historical context will help you put this literary piece into the proper perspective of what is taking place.

The use of this study guide will save you the hours of preparation time that would ordinarily be required to arrive at a complete grasp of this work of literature. You will be well prepared for classroom discussions, homework, and exams. The guidelines that are included for writing papers and reports on various topics will prepare you for any added work which may be assigned.

The **MAXnotes** will take your grades "to the max."

Dr. Max Fogiel
Program Director

Contents

**Each Scene includes List of Characters,
Summary, Analysis, Study Questions and
Answers, and Suggested Essay Topics.**

SECTION ONE

Introduction

The Life and Work of William Shakespeare

The details of William Shakespeare's life are sketchy, mostly mere surmise based upon court or other clerical records. His parents, John and Mary (Arden), were married about 1557; she was of the landed gentry, and he was a yeoman—a glover and commodities merchant. By 1568, John had risen through the ranks of town government and held the position of high bailiff, which was a position similar to mayor. William, the eldest son and the third of eight children, was born in 1564, probably on April 23, several days before his baptism on April 26 in Stratford-upon-Avon. Shakespeare is also believed to have died on the same date—April 23—in 1616.

It is believed that William attended the local grammar school in Stratford where his parents lived, and that he studied primarily Latin, rhetoric, logic, and literature. Shakespeare probably left school at age 15, which was the norm, to take a job, especially since this was the period of his father's financial difficulty. At age 18 (1582), William married Anne Hathaway, a local farmer's daughter who was eight years his senior. Their first daughter (Susanna) was born six months later (1583), and twins Judith and Hamnet were born in 1585.

Shakespeare's life can be divided into three periods: the first 20 years in Stratford, which include his schooling, early marriage, and fatherhood; the next 25 years as an actor and playwright in London; and the last five in retirement in Stratford where he enjoyed moderate wealth gained from his theatrical successes. The years linking the first two periods are marked by a lack of information about Shakespeare, and are often referred to as the "dark years."

At some point during the "dark years," Shakespeare began his career with a London theatrical company, perhaps in 1589, for he was already an actor and playwright of some note by 1592. Shakespeare apparently wrote and acted for numerous theatrical companies, including Pembroke's Men, and Strange's Men, which later became the Chamberlain's Men, with whom he remained for the rest of his career.

In 1592, the Plague closed the theaters for about two years, and Shakespeare turned to writing book-length narrative poetry. Most notable were "Venus and Adonis" and "The Rape of Lucrece," both of which were dedicated to the Earl of Southampton, whom scholars accept as Shakespeare's friend and benefactor despite a lack of documentation. During this same period, Shakespeare was writing his sonnets, which are more likely signs of the time's fashion rather than actual love poems detailing any particular relationship. He returned to playwriting when theaters reopened in 1594, and did not continue to write poetry. His sonnets were published without his consent in 1609, shortly before his retirement.

Amid all of his success, Shakespeare suffered the loss of his only son, Hamnet, who died in 1596 at the age of 11. But Shakespeare's career continued unabated, and in London in 1599, he became one of the partners in the new Globe Theater, which was built by the Chamberlain's Men.

Shakespeare wrote very little after 1612, which was the year he completed *Henry VIII*. It was during a performance of this play in 1613 that the Globe caught fire and burned to the ground. Sometime between 1610 and 1613, Shakespeare returned to Stratford, where he owned a large house and property, to spend his remaining years with his family.

William Shakespeare died on April 23, 1616, and was buried two days later in the chancel of Holy Trinity Church, where he had been baptized exactly 52 years earlier. His literary legacy included 37 plays, 154 sonnets, and five major poems.

Incredibly, most of Shakespeare's plays had never been published in anything except pamphlet form, and were simply extant as acting scripts stored at the Globe. Theater scripts were not regarded as literary works of art, but only the basis for the performance. Plays were simply a popular form of entertainment for all layers of society in Shakespeare's time. Only the efforts of two of Shakespeare's company, John Heminges and Henry Condell, preserved his 36 plays (minus *Pericles*, the thirty-seventh).

Shakespeare's Language

Shakespeare's language can create a strong pang of intimidation, even fear, in a large number of modern-day readers. Fortunately, however, this need not be the case. All that is needed to master the art of reading Shakespeare is to practice the techniques of unraveling uncommonly-structured sentences and to become familiar with the poetic use of uncommon words. We must realize that during the 400-year span between Shakespeare's time and our own, both the way we live and speak has changed. Although most of his vocabulary is in use today, some of it is obsolete, and what may be most confusing is that some of his words are used today, but with slightly different or totally different meanings. On the stage, actors readily dissolve these language stumbling blocks. They study Shakespeare's dialogue and express it dramatically in word and in action so that its meaning is graphically enacted. If the reader studies Shakespeare's lines as an actor does, looking up and reflecting upon the meaning of unfamiliar words until real voice is discovered, he or she will suddenly experience the excitement, the depth and the sheer poetry of what these characters say.

Shakespeare's Sentences

In English, or any other language, the meaning of a sentence greatly depends upon where each word is placed in that sentence. "The child hurt the mother" and "The mother hurt the child" have opposite meanings, even though the words are the same, simply because the words are arranged differently. Because word position is so integral to English, the reader will find unfamiliar word arrangements confusing, even difficult to understand. Since Shakespeare's plays are poetic dramas, he often shifts from average word arrangements to the strikingly unusual so that the line will conform to the desired poetic rhythm. Often, too, Shakespeare employs unusual word order to afford a character his own specific style of speaking.

Today, English sentence structure follows a sequence of subject first, verb second, and an optional object third. Shakespeare, however, often places the verb before the subject, which reads, "Speaks he" rather than "He speaks." Solanio speaks with this inverted structure in *The Merchant of Venice* stating, "I should be still/ Plucking the grass to know where sits the wind" (Bevington edition, I, i, ll.17-19), while today's standard English word order would have the clause at the end of this line read, "where the wind sits." "Wind" is the subject of this clause, and "sits" is the verb. Bassanio's words in Act Two also exemplify this inversion: "And in such eyes as ours appear not faults" (II, ii, l. 184). In our normal word order, we would say, "Faults do not appear in eyes such as ours," with "faults" as the subject in both Shakespeare's word order and ours.

Inversions like these are not troublesome, but when Shakespeare positions the predicate adjective or the object before the subject and verb, we are sometimes surprised. For example, rather than "I saw him," Shakespeare may use a structure such as "Him I saw." Similarly, "Cold the morning is" would be used for our "The morning is cold." Lady Macbeth demonstrates this inversion as she speaks of her husband: "Glamis thou art, and Cawdor, and shalt be/What thou art promised" (Macbeth, I, v, ll. 14-15). In current English word order, this quote would begin, "Thou art Glamis, and Cawdor."

In addition to inversions, Shakespeare purposefully keeps words apart that we generally keep together. To illustrate, consider Bassanio's humble admission in *The Merchant of Venice*: "I owe you much, and, like a wilful youth,/That which I owe is lost" (I, i, ll. 146-147). The phrase, "like a wilful youth," separates the regular sequence of "I owe you much" and "That which I owe is lost." To understand more clearly this type of passage, the reader could rearrange these word groups into our conventional order: I owe you much and I wasted what you gave me because I was young and impulsive. While these rearranged clauses will sound like normal English, and will be simpler to understand, they will no longer have the desired poetic rhythm, and the emphasis will now be on the wrong words.

As we read Shakespeare, we will find words that are separated by long, interruptive statements. Often subjects are separated from verbs, and verbs are separated from objects. These long interruptions can be used to give a character dimension or to add an element of suspense. For example, in *Romeo and Juliet* Benvolio describes both Romeo's moodiness and his own sensitive and thoughtful nature:

> I, measuring his affections by my own,
> Which then most sought, where most might not be found,
> Being one too many by my weary self,
> Pursu'd my humour, not pursuing his,
> And gladly shunn'd who gladly fled from me. (I, i, ll. 126-130)

In this passage, the subject "I" is distanced from its verb "Pursu'd." The long interruption serves to provide information which is integral to the plot. Another example, taken from *Hamlet*, is the ghost, Hamlet's father, who describes Hamlet's uncle, Claudius, as

> ...that incestuous, that adulterate beast,
> With witchcraft of his wit, with traitorous gifts—
> O wicked wit and gifts, that have the power
> So to seduce—won to his shameful lust
> The will of my most seeming virtuous queen. (I, v, ll. 43-47)

From this we learn that Prince Hamlet's mother is the victim of an evil seduction and deception. The delay between the subject, "beast," and the verb, "won," creates a moment of tension filled with the image of a cunning predator waiting for the right moment to spring into attack. This interruptive passage allows the play to unfold crucial information and thus to build the tension necessary to produce a riveting drama.

While at times these long delays are merely for decorative purposes, they are often used to narrate a particular situation or to enhance character development. As *Antony and Cleopatra* opens, an interruptive passage occurs in the first few lines. Although the delay is not lengthy, Philo's words vividly portray Antony's military prowess while they also reveal the immediate concern of the drama. Antony is distracted from his career, and is now focused on Cleopatra:

>   ...those goodly eyes,
> That o'er the files and musters of the war
> Have glow'd like plated Mars, now bend, now turn
> The office and devotion of their view
> Upon a tawny front.... (I, i, ll. 2-6)

Whereas Shakespeare sometimes heaps detail upon detail, his sentences are often elliptical, that is, they omit words we expect in written English sentences. In fact, we often do this in our spoken conversations. For instance, we say, "You see that?" when we really mean, "Did you see that?" Reading poetry or listening to lyrics in music conditions us to supply the omitted words and it makes us more comfortable reading this type of dialogue. Consider one passage in *The Merchant of Venice* where Antonio's friends ask him why he seems so sad and Solanio tells Antonio, "Why, then you are in love" (I, i, l. 46). When Antonio denies this, Solanio responds, "Not in love neither?" (I, i, l. 47). The word "you" is omitted but understood despite the confusing double negative.

In addition to leaving out words, Shakespeare often uses intentionally vague language, a strategy which taxes the reader's attentiveness. In *Antony and Cleopatra*, Cleopatra, upset that Antony is leaving for Rome after learning that his wife died in battle, convinces him to stay in Egypt:

>   Sir, you and I must part, but that's not it:
> Sir you and I have lov'd, but there's not it;
> That you know well, something it is I would—
> O, my oblivion is a very Antony,
> And I am all forgotten. (I, iii, ll. 87-91, emphasis added)

In line 89, "...something it is I would" suggests that there is something that she would want to say, do, or have done. The intentional vagueness leaves us, and certainly Antony, to wonder. Though this sort of writing may appear lackadaisical for all that it leaves out, here the vagueness functions to portray Cleopatra as rhetorically sophisticated. Similarly, when asked what thing a crocodile is (meaning Antony himself who is being compared to a

crocodile), Antony slyly evades the question by giving a vague reply:

> It is shap'd, sir, like itself, and it is as broad as it hath
> breadth. It is just so high as it is, and moves with it own
> organs. It lives by that which nourisheth it, and, the
> elements once out of it, it transmigrates. (II, vii, ll. 43-46)

This kind of evasiveness, or doubletalk, occurs often in Shakespeare's writing and requires extra patience on the part of the reader.

Shakespeare's Words

As we read Shakespeare's plays, we will encounter uncommon
words. Many of these words are not in use today. As *Romeo and
Juliet* opens, we notice words like "shrift" (confession) and
"holidame" (a holy relic). Words like these should be explained in
notes to the text. Shakespeare also employs words which we still
use, though with different meaning. For example, in *The Merchant
of Venice* "caskets" refer to small, decorative chests for holding jew-
els. However, modern readers may think of a large cask instead of
the smaller, diminutive casket.

Another trouble modern readers will have with Shakespeare's
English is with words that are still in use today, but which mean
something different in Elizabethan use. In *The Merchant of Venice*,
Shakespeare uses the word "straight" (as in "straight away") where
we would say "immediately." Here, the modern reader is unlikely
to carry away the wrong message, however, since the modern
meaning will simply make no sense. In this case, textual notes will
clarify a phrase's meaning. To cite another example, in *Romeo and
Juliet*, after Mercutio dies, Romeo states that the "black fate on moe
days doth depend" (emphasis added). In this case, "depend" really
means "impend."

Shakespeare's Wordplay

All of Shakespeare's works exhibit his mastery of playing with
language and with such variety that many people have authored
entire books on this subject alone. Shakespeare's most frequently
used types of wordplay are common: metaphors, similes, synec-

doche and metonymy, personification, allusion, and puns. It is
when Shakespeare violates the normal use of these devices, or rhetorical figures, that the language becomes confusing.

A metaphor is a comparison in which an object or idea is replaced by another object or idea with common attributes. For example, in *Macbeth* a murderer tells Macbeth that Banquo has been
murdered, as directed, but that his son, Fleance, escaped, having
witnessed his father's murder. Fleance, now a threat to Macbeth,
is described as a serpent:

> There the grown serpent lies, the worm that's fled
> Hath nature that in time will venom breed,
> No teeth for the present. (III, iv, ll. 29-31, emphasis added)

Similes, on the other hand, compare objects or ideas while
using the words "like" or "as." In *Romeo and Juliet,* Romeo tells Juliet
that "Love goes toward love as schoolboys from their books" (II, ii,
l. 156). Such similes often give way to more involved comparisons,
"extended similes." For example, Juliet tells Romeo:

> 'Tis almost morning, I would have thee gone,
> And yet no farther than a wonton's bird,
> That lets it hop a little from his hand
> Like a poor prisoner in his twisted gyves,
> And with silken thread plucks it back again,
> So loving-jealous of his liberty.
> (II, ii, ll. 176-181, emphasis added)

An epic simile, a device borrowed from heroic poetry, is an extended simile that builds into an even more elaborate comparison. In *Macbeth*, Macbeth describes King Duncan's virtues with an
angelic, celestial simile and then drives immediately into another
simile that redirects us into a vision of warfare and destruction:

> ...Besides this Duncan
> Hath borne his faculties so meek, hath been
> So clear in his great office, that his virtues
> Will plead like angels, trumpet-tongued, against

> The deep damnation of his taking-off;
> And pity, like a naked new-born babe,
> Striding the blast, or heaven's cherubim, horsed
> Upon the sightless couriers of the air,
> Shall blow the horrid deed in every eye,
> That tears shall drown the wind....
> (I, vii, ll. 16-25, emphasis added)

Shakespeare employs other devices, like synecdoche and metonymy, to achieve "verbal economy," or using one or two words to express more than one thought. Synecdoche is a figure of speech using a part for the whole. An example of synecdoche is using the word boards to imply a stage. Boards are only a small part of the materials that make up a stage, however, the term boards has become a colloquial synonym for stage. Metonymy is a figure of speech using the name of one thing for that of another which it is associated. An example of metonymy is using crown to mean the king (as used in the sentence "These lands belong to the crown"). Since a crown is associated with or an attribute of the king, the word crown has become a metonymy for the king. It is important to understand that every metonymy is a synecdoche, but not every synecdoche is a metonymy. This is rule is true because a metonymy must not only be a part of the root word, making a synecdoche, but also be a unique attribute of or associated with the root word.

Synecdoche and metonymy in Shakespeare's works is often very confusing to a new student because he creates uses for words that they usually do not perform. This technique is often complicated and yet very subtle, which makes it difficult of a new student to dissect and understand. An example of these devices in one of Shakespeare's plays can be found in *The Merchant of Venice* . In warning his daughter, Jessica, to ignore the Christian revelries in the streets below, Shylock says:

> Lock up my doors; and when you hear the drum
> And the vile squealing of the wry-necked fife,
> Clamber not you up to the casements then. . .
> (I, v, ll. 30-32)

The phrase of importance in this quote is "the wry-necked fife." When a reader examines this phrase it does not seem to make sense; a fife is a cylinder-shaped instrument, there is no part of it that can be called a neck. The phrase then must be taken to refer to the fife-player, who has to twist his or her neck to play the fife. Fife, therefore, is a synecdoche for fife-player, much as boards is for stage. The trouble with understanding this phrase is that "vile squealing" logically refers to the sound of the fife, not the fife-player, and the reader might be led to take fife as the instrument because of the parallel reference to "drum" in the previous line. The best solution to this quandary is that Shakespeare uses the word fife to refer to both the instrument and the player. Both the player and the instrument are needed to complete the wordplay in this phrase, which, though difficult to understand to new readers, cannot be seen as a flaw since Shakespeare manages to convey two meanings with one word. This remarkable example of synecdoche illuminates Shakespeare's mastery of "verbal economy."

Shakespeare also uses vivid and imagistic wordplay through personification, in which human capacities and behaviors are attributed to inanimate objects. Bassanio, in *The Merchant of Venice*, almost speechless when Portia promises to marry him and share all her worldly wealth, states "my blood speaks to you in my veins..." (III, ii, l. 176). How deeply he must feel since even his blood can speak. Similarly, Portia, learning of the penalty that Antonio must pay for defaulting on his debt, tells Salerio, "There are some shrewd contents in yond same paper / That steals the color from Bassanio's cheek" (III, ii, ll. 243-244).

Another important facet of Shakespeare's rhetorical repertoire is his use of allusion. An allusion is a reference to another author or to an historical figure or event. Very often Shakespeare alludes to the heroes and heroines of Ovid's *Metamorphoses*. For example, in Cymbeline an entire room is decorated with images illustrating the stories from this classical work, and the heroine, Imogen, has been reading from this text. Similarly, in *Titus Andronicus* characters not only read directly from the *Metamorphoses*, but a subplot re-enacts one of the *Metamorphoses's* most famous stories, the rape and mutilation of Philomel.

Another way Shakespeare uses allusion is to drop names of mythological, historical and literary figures. In *The Taming of the Shrew*, for instance, Petruchio compares Katharina, the woman whom he is courting, to Diana (II, i, l. 55), the virgin goddess, in order to suggest that Katharina is a man-hater. At times, Shakespeare will allude to well-known figures without so much as mentioning their names. In *Twelfth Night*, for example, though the Duke and Valentine are ostensibly interested in Olivia, a rich countess, Shakespeare asks his audience to compare the Duke's emotional turmoil to the plight of Acteon, whom the goddess Diana transforms into a deer to be hunted and killed by Acteon's own dogs:

Duke: That instant was I turn'd into a hart,
              And my desires, like fell and cruel hounds,
              E'er since pursue me.
              [...]
Valentine: But like a cloistress she will veiled walk,
              And water once a day her chamber round....
              (I, i, l. 20 ff.)

Shakespeare's use of puns spotlights his exceptional wit. His comedies in particular are loaded with puns, usually of a sexual nature. Puns work through the ambiguity that results when multiple senses of a word are evoked; homophones often cause this sort of ambiguity. In *Antony and Cleopatra*, Enobarbus believes "there is mettle in death" (I, ii, l. 146), meaning that there is "courage" in death; at the same time, mettle suggests the homophone metal, referring to swords made of metal causing death. In early editions of Shakespeare's work there was no distinction made between the two words. Antony puns on the word "earing," (I, ii, ll. 112-114) meaning both plowing (as in rooting out weeds) and hearing: he angrily sends away a messenger, not wishing to hear the message from his wife, Fulvia: "...O then we bring forth weeds,/ when our quick minds lie still, and our ills told us/Is as our earing." If ill-natured news is planted in one's "hearing," it will render an "earing" (harvest) of ill-natured thoughts. A particularly clever pun, also in *Antony and Cleopatra*, stands out after Antony's troops have fought Octavius's men in Egypt: "We have beat him to his camp.

Run one before,/And let the queen know of our gests" (IV, viii, ll. 1-2). Here "gests" means deeds (in this case, deeds of battle); it is also a pun on "guests," as though Octavius' slain soldiers were to be guests when buried in Egypt.

One should note that Elizabethan pronunciation was in several cases different from our own. Thus, modern readers, especially Americans, will miss out on the many puns based on homophones. The textual notes will point up many of these "lost" puns, however.

Shakespeare's sexual innuendoes can be either clever or tedious depending upon the speaker and situation. The modern reader should recall that sexuality in Shakespeare's time was far more complex than in ours and that characters may refer to such things as masturbation and homosexual activity. Textual notes in some editions will point out these puns but rarely explain them. An example of a sexual pun or innuendo can be found in *The Merchant of Venice* when Portia and Nerissa are discussing Portia's past suitors using innuendo to tell of their sexual prowess:

Portia:	I pray thee, overname them, and as thou namest them, I will describe them, and according to my description level at my affection.
Nerrisa:	First, there is the Neapolitan prince.
Portia:	Ay, that's a colt indeed, for he doth nothing but talk of his horse, and he makes it a great appropriation to his own good parts that he can shoe him himself. I am much afeard my lady his mother played false with the smith.
	(I, ii, ll. 35-45)

The "Neapolitan prince" is given a grade of an inexperienced youth when Portia describes him as a "colt." The prince is thought to be inexperienced because he did nothing but "talk of his horse" (a pun for his penis) and his other great attributes. Portia goes on to say that the prince boasted that he could "shoe him [his horse] himself," a possible pun meaning that the prince was very proud that he could masturbate. Finally, Portia makes an attack upon the prince's mother, saying that "my lady his mother played false with the smith," a pun to say his mother must have committed adultery with a blacksmith to give birth to such a vulgar man having an obsession with "shoeing his horse."

It is worth mentioning that Shakespeare gives the reader hints when his characters might be using puns and innuendoes. In *The Merchant of Venice*, Portia's lines are given in prose when she is joking, or engaged in bawdy conversations. Later on the reader will notice that Portia's lines are rhymed in poetry, such as when she is talking in court or to Bassanio. This is Shakespeare's way of letting the reader know when Portia is jesting and when she is serious.

Shakespeare's Dramatic Verse

Finally, the reader will notice that some lines are actually rhymed verse while others are in verse without rhyme; and much of Shakespeare's drama is in prose. Shakespeare usually has his lovers speak in the language of love poetry which uses rhymed couplets. The archetypal example of this comes, of course, from *Romeo and Juliet*:

> The grey-ey'd morn smiles on the frowning night,
> Check'ring the eastern clouds with streaks of light,
> And fleckled darkness like a drunkard reels
> From forth day's path and Titan's fiery wheels.
> (II, iii, ll. 1-4)

Here it is ironic that Friar Lawrence should speak these lines since he is not the one in love. He, therefore, appears buffoonish and out of touch with reality. Shakespeare often has his characters speak in rhymed verse to let the reader know that the character is acting in jest, and vice-versa.

Perhaps the majority of Shakespeare's lines are in blank verse, a form of poetry which does not use rhyme (hence the name blank) but still employs a rhythm native to the English language, iambic pentameter, where every second syllable in a line of ten syllables receives stress. Consider the following verses from *Hamlet*, and note the accents and the lack of end-rhyme:

> The síngle ánd pecúliar lífe is bóund
> With áll the stréngth and ármor óf the mínd
> (III, iii, ll. 12-13)

The final syllable of these verses receives stress and is said to have a hard, or "strong," ending. A soft ending, also said to be "weak," receives no stress. In *The Tempest*, Shakespeare uses a soft ending to shape a verse that demonstrates through both sound (meter) and sense the capacity of the feminine to propagate:

> and thén I lóv'd thee
> And shów'd thee áll the quálitíes o' th' ísle,
> The frésh spríngs, bríne-pits, bárren pláce and fértile.
> (I, ii, ll. 338-40)

The first and third of these lines here have soft endings.

In general, Shakespeare saves blank verse for his characters of noble birth. Therefore, it is significant when his lofty characters speak in prose. Prose holds a special place in Shakespeare's dialogues; he uses it to represent the speech habits of the common people. Not only do lowly servants and common citizens speak in prose, but important, lower class figures also use this fun, at times ribald variety of speech. Though Shakespeare crafts some very ornate lines in verse, his prose can be equally daunting, for some of his characters may speechify and break into doubletalk in their attempts to show sophistication. A clever instance of this comes when the Third Citizen in Coriolanus refers to the people's paradoxical lack of power when they must elect Coriolanus as their new leader once Coriolanus has orated how he has courageously fought for them in battle:

> We have power in ourselves to do it, but it is
> a power that we have no power to do; for if he show us his
> wounds and tell us his deeds, we are to put our tongues
> into those wounds and speak for them; so, if he tell us his
> noble deeds, we must also tell him our noble acceptance
> of them. Ingratitude is monstrous, and for the multitude
> to be ingrateful were to make a monster of the multitude,

of the which we, being members, should bring ourselves
to be monstrous members.
(II, ii, ll. 3-13)

Notice that this passage contains as many metaphors, hideous
though they be, as any other passage in Shakespeare's dramatic verse.

When reading Shakespeare, paying attention to characters who
suddenly break into rhymed verse, or who slip into prose after
speaking in blank verse, will heighten your awareness of a
character's mood and personal development. For instance, in
Antony and Cleopatra, the famous military leader Marcus Antony
usually speaks in blank verse, but also speaks in fits of prose (II, iii,
ll. 43-46) once his masculinity and authority have been questioned.
Similarly, in *Timon of Athens*, after the wealthy lord Timon aban-
dons the city of Athens to live in a cave, he harangues anyone whom
he encounters in prose (IV, iii, l. 331 ff.). In contrast, the reader
should wonder why the bestial Caliban in *The Tempest* speaks in
blank verse rather than in prose.

Implied Stage Action

When we read a Shakespearean play, we are reading a performance text. Actors interact through dialogue, but at the same time
these actors cry, gesticulate, throw tantrums, pick up daggers, and
compulsively wash murderous "blood" from their hands. Some of
the action that takes place on stage is explicitly stated in stage directions. However, some of the stage activity is couched within the
dialogue itself. Attentiveness to these cues is important as one conceives how to visualize the action. When Iago in *Othello* feigns concern for Cassio whom he himself has stabbed, he calls to the
surrounding men, "Come, come:/Lend me a light" (V, i, ll. 86-87). It
is almost sure that one of the actors involved will bring him a torch
or lantern. In the same play, Emilia, Desdemona's maidservant, asks
if she should fetch her lady's nightgown and Desdemona replies,
"No, unpin me here" (IV, iii, l. 37). In *Macbeth*, after killing Duncan,
Macbeth brings the murder weapon back with him. When he tells
his wife that he cannot return to the scene and place the daggers to
suggest that the king's guards murdered Duncan, she castigates him:
"Infirm of purpose/Give me the daggers. The sleeping and the dead

are but as pictures" (II, ii, ll. 50-52). As she exits, it is easy to visualize Lady Macbeth grabbing the daggers from her husband.

For 400 years, readers have found it greatly satisfying to work with all aspects of Shakespeare's language—the implied stage action, word choice, sentence structure, and wordplay—until all aspects come to life. Just as seeing a fine performance of a Shakespearean play is exciting, staging the play in one's own mind's eye, and revisiting lines to enrich the sense of the action, will enhance one's appreciation of Shakespeare's extraordinary literary and dramatic achievements.

Historical Background

Although there has been much debate, Shakespeare is now believed to have composed *The Taming of the Shrew* between 1592 and 1594. Although a play named *The Taming of A Shrew* was published first in the so-called "bad quarto" of 1594, Shakespeare's own version was not published until 1623 when the First Folio of his works was compiled. The pirated version is thought to be a fast transcription, not without some embellishment, of Shakespeare's play as it was performed.

The first *known* performance of *The Taming of the Shrew* was held at Newington Butts on June 13, 1594 by Shakespeare's own company, the Chamberlain's Men. Shakespeare himself played the part of Vincentio (a confined role) alongside the very popular actor Richard Burbage, who played Lucentio. However, there is a reference (not a record) in the "bad quarto" to earlier performances by the Earl of Pembroke's Men, a troop which disbanded in 1594 due to financial troubles.

The Newington Butts stage was located one mile south of London Bridge in one of the Liberties, so called because they lay outside of the city limits where strict municipal laws did not affect the theater. Londoners regularly traveled outside the city proper to see their favorite plays, except during plague years when the theaters were closed for the public's safety. The Globe, Shakespeare's famous playhouse, was likewise located in the Liberties. When it burned down, Shakespeare's company was forced to move into London to Blackfriars and other playhouses.

The Taming of the Shrew enjoyed instant popularity. Its pirated copy was republished in 1596 and 1607. Shakespeare's version of the play was even performed in the court of Charles I by the King's Company on November 16, 1633 at St. James Palace.

It should be noted that all plays performed before 1642 required an all-male cast since women were not allowed on stage. Only after the restoration of the Stuart monarchy in 1660 were women permitted to act. In its first known performance, for example, the actors Alexander Cooke, Robert Goffe, and Samuel Gilburne played the parts of Katharina, Bianca, and the Widow respectively.

Shakespeare's play has maintained its popularity right through to our own time, but not in its original form. Various playwrights have adapted *Shrew* to suit the taste of their times. The original play has been transformed from comedy into both farce and tragedy. This is not surprising since *Shrew* contains elements of each.

Three versions of the play have outstripped Shakespeare's original in popularity. Its biggest success has been David Garrick's adaptation titled *Catharine and Petruchio*, first staged in 1754 but running into the next century in over 300 performances. Garrick's version employed only the main plot of Shakespeare's play, as the title reflects, and it was used only as an afterpiece to a play that received first billing.

Another great success was John Lacy's adaptation named *Sauny the Scot*, first performed in 1667 but published later in 1698. Lacy's version omits the framing plot but stays close to Shakespeare's original and the farcical nature of the character Grumio, Petruchio's idiotic servant. Though this play also was copied and adapted, Shakespeare's original, except for the Induction, has finally come back into vogue in this century. It has been filmed several times. Unfortunately for the dedicated student of Shakespeare, only one film version has ever employed the framing plot of Sly, and its availability is uncertain. It was directed by Henri Desfontaines for Eclipse Films, and released in the United States in 1911.

Currently, *The Taming of the Shrew* ranks alongside *The Tempest* in popularity, though several Shakespearean plays enjoy greater success, such as *As You Like It, Midsummer Night's Dream, Othello, Romeo and Juliet,* and *Twelfth Night.* Of course, *Hamlet, Macbeth* and *King Lear* are performed far more than any of Shakespeare's plays.

Master List of Characters

Petruchio—*the clever but rough man who tames the "shrew" to be, his wife*

Katharina—*the shrew; a sharp-tongued woman who will not take a husband; She finally capitulates to the overpowering Petruchio and becomes the model wife.*

Bianca—*Katharina's beautiful younger sister who cannot marry until a man weds Katharina*

Lucentio—*a young man who wants to marry Bianca; disguises himself as , Cambio, a teacher, to woo Bianca covertly*

Baptista—*the wealthy father of Katharina and Bianca*

Gremio—*an old man and suitor to Bianca.*

Hortensio—*disguises himself as Litio , a musician, in order to woo Bianca covertly; breaks off his suit when she favors Cambio, and marries a wealthy widow instead*

Vincentio—*Lucentio's father; a wealthy merchant who resides in Pisa*

Tranio—*Lucentio's servant who disguises himself as his master and comes to Baptista to court Bianca on Lucentio's behalf*

Biondello—*servant to Lucentio who slanders his father, Vincentio*

Grumio—*patient servant to Petruchio*

Pedant—*is disguised as Lucentio's father, Vincentio*

Widow—*marries Hortensio and surprises everyone at the play's end by being more shrewish than Katharina*

Christopher Sly—*a common tinker, fooled into believing that he is a nobleman*

Lord—*a nobleman who plays an elaborate joke on the unsuspecting Christopher Sly*

Page—*Bartholomew, probably a teenage boy; His master dresses him up as a woman to play the wife of Christopher Sly.*

Summary of the Play

The principal five acts of the play are preceded by an Induction. Thus the five acts really compose a play-within-a-play, Shakespearean device. In the Induction, a nobleman out for a laugh puts a drunken tinker and vagrant, Christopher Sly, into bed. He awakens to find a woman calling herself his wife. The wife, who is really the lord's page dressed as a woman, claims that Sly is a lord. Sly wants his wife to join him in his bed, but she puts him off by asking him to watch a play performed by a newly arrived theater company.

In the central play itself, Lucentio, a young man from Pisa, arrives in Padua to attend its famous university. He quickly becomes enamored of the fair Bianca, who is also pursued by two other men, Gremio and Hortensio.

Bianca's father, Baptista, will not give away his younger daughter before the elder Katharina—the shrew—is wedded, so Hortensio arranges for his friend, the surly Petruchio, to woo Katharina. Meanwhile, Lucentio disguises himself as one "Cambio," a teacher of Latin, in order to woo Bianca. His servant, Tranio, arrives dressed as his master to bargain with Baptista for Bianca's hand in marriage. Hortensio also comes to woo Bianca disguised as the musician, Litio. Bianca favors the younger of the two, and secretly promises to marry Lucentio.

Petruchio makes his suit to Katharina, who vehemently rejects him. Petruchio uses clever repartee to trick Kate into agreeing to marry him. When Petruchio returns to Padua a few days later to wed Kate, he appears slovenly and vulgar. After running out on his own wedding banquet, Petruchio takes Kate to his home in nearby Verona. He subjects her to humiliation by not allowing her to eat, sleep or wear proper clothing for her visit back home. Gradually, Kate submits to this form of "taming." She swears that the sun shines even though it is night, just to please her new husband.

Meanwhile, to secure his marriage with Bianca, Lucentio disguises a pedant as his father. But Vincentio, Lucentio's real father, interrupts the proceedings. After some dispute, father and son are reconciled, and Vincentio consents to the marriage.

Petruchio and Kate return to Padua to attend the wedding banquet of Lucentio and Bianca. Hortensio and his new wife, the widow, are also present. In order to show how masterfully he has tamed his shrew, Petruchio sets up a wager among the grooms to find out whose bride will obey most readily. Each man must call on his wife to attend him.

When summoned, the widow and Bianca both spurn their masters. Kate immediately appears, and also brings out the other two wives. Kate then proceeds to harangue the two stubborn women for neglecting their masters. All of the venom that Kate had once used upon her suitors is now turned against the widow and Bianca. All concede that Petruchio has successfully tamed his shrew.

Estimated Reading Time

Readers will be happy to find that *The Taming of the Shrew* is one of Shakespeare's most enjoyable and easy-to-read plays. Allow anywhere from three to four hours to read through this comedy. Readers may want to slow down for the details of character switching and disguises. Selecting an edition with good footnotes to the text is always a good policy. Possible choices are the Riverside and Bevington editions or those published by the Oxford, Cambridge and Methuen (Arden Shakespeare) presses. Readers will note that some lines are in Latin. Although most of these lines have no direct bearing on the play, some students might wish to understand why Shakespeare chose to quote the Latin author, Ovid. There are also many references to mythological persons in *The Taming of the Shrew*, as in most Shakespearean plays. Again, a footnoted text will help the reader ponder what Shakespeare intends by comparing characters to certain legendary heroes or victims.

Students may also want to view the most recent American film version of *The Taming of the Shrew*, starring Elizabeth Taylor and Richard Burton. Beware, however, that all available film versions leave out the Induction.

The Induction

The Induction, Scene 1

New Characters:

Christopher Sly: *a drunken tinker (pot-mender) who becomes the subject of a nobleman's joke*

Hostess: *the innkeeper who must run after a constable in order to force Sly to pay for damaged goods*

Lord: *a nobleman who finds Sly asleep and decides to play an elaborate joke at Sly's expense*

Servants and **huntsmen:** *minor players who serve the Lord*

Players: *members of a traveling theater company*

Summary

The play begins with a quarrel between an innkeeper and a drunken tinker, Christopher Sly, who has presumably consumed too much ale and has broken some glasses. When Sly refuses to pay for what he has broken, the hostess goes off in search of a constable, and Sly falls into a drunken sleep.

A nobleman, returning from hunting, finds Sly asleep in front of an English alehouse. After berating Sly's bestial appearance, the Lord decides to "practice" on him by dressing Sly up as a nobleman and placing him in the Lord's own house, which is just nearby. The Lord arranges for his own servants to convince Sly that he has

always been a nobleman, but one who has of late fallen into a dementia wherein he only raved that he was a commoner.

A group of players arrives at the Lord's home and asks permission to perform for him. The Lord claims to recognize a member of the group from a previous performance, but obviously errs. Nonetheless, the Lord agrees to the performance, which he intends as entertainment for Sly. He instructs the players to ignore Sly, who might act strangely.

With the players gone, the Lord instructs one of his servants to dress up his page, Bartholomew, to play the noble wife of Sly. The Lord further stipulates that Bartholomew should cry like a woman for joy when Sly wakes up from the supposed dementia. To enjoy his joke all the more, the Lord plans to be present when Sly wakes up. He also comments that his austere presence will calm any mirth in his servants that would ruin the joke.

Analysis

The Induction to *The Taming of the Shrew* is often omitted from film versions and even published discussions of the play. Its importance and relevance to the central five acts of the play, which actually constitute a play-within-a-play, is often missed by readers who understandably prefer the fast and funny action of the later scenes. Genius writer that he was, Shakespeare uses the Induction to present two key thematic elements that assume importance in the central five acts.

The opening to the Induction emphasizes the differences between social classes in Shakespeare's England. In order of importance, there appear a member of the aristocracy (the Lord), the bourgeoisie (the hostess/innkeeper), and the proletariat (the tinker, Christopher Sly). The players belong to a new class of workers in England, and have no fixed place in this social hierarchy; they might be thought of socially as a wild card in the social strata of the English Renaissance.

The tension between classes is most readily visible in the conflict between the hostess and Christopher Sly. Notice how Sly claims that his family "came in with Richard [the] Conqueror." Here, Sly intends to allude to the invasion of William the Conqueror, the legendary prince from Normandy who brought his court with him to England and replaced an Anglo-Saxon nobility with a French-speaking aristocracy. However Sly blunders the name of the famous king, revealing his own pretentious and unsophisticated nature.

In comparison to the culturally refined Lord, Sly appears a "monstrous beast" or "swine." The Lord plans to entertain himself by putting on a performance of his own, one in which he plays up to the pretentions of the commoner Sly, who just tries to associate himself with England's "old money" nobility.

By dressing up Sly in a nobleman's clothes, the Lord is taking an extreme license. A few years before Shakespeare wrote this play, Elizabeth I had passed her first of several *sumptuary laws* which prohibited people from dressing above their "station," or place, in English society. This meant that a bricklayer could not wear the clothes of a merchant. Similarly, a merchant could not don the rich apparel of an aristocrat. Since dressing down implied the *loss* of social privilege, that practice was not officially discouraged.

Elizabethan theater players, no less than other English citizens, had to conform to the same laws, but special privileges were accorded to certain theatrical companies so actors could portray monarchs and aristocrats. One can see now that it is no accident that Shakespeare has a band of players intrude upon the Lord's home at the very moment the Lord plans to make a performer out of his unwitting guest.

The scene ends with the Lord giving instructions for his page to dress up as a woman and pretend to be Sly's wife. This element of the plot points directly to the practice of male cross-dressing on the Elizabethan and Jacobean stages. ("Jacobean" refers to the reign of James I.) Originally due to religious concerns, but later due to social custom, women were barred from the stage. Only with the revival of the theater at the English Restoration in 1660 were women allowed on stage. In their absence, boys were hired to play the roles of women in dramatic productions. A relic of this practice can still be seen in various British comedies, most notably "Monty Python's Flying Circus."

It is no accident that the Lord in *The Taming of the Shrew* asks his page, rather than a grown man, to play the part of Sly's wife. We call this type of "coincidence" in the theater "self-consciousness," for the audience's attention is pointed toward the conventions of the stage rather than the action of the plot.

The ability to act a part, the central theme of the entire play, becomes crucial when the Lord focuses on Bartholomew's ability to cry at will. This two-sided gesture points, on the one hand, to a boy's ability to portray a woman, and, on the other, to a woman's ability to cry on command. The Lord's comment about a woman's tears introduces the issue of whether human behavior is natural or actually adapted to suit the necessities of social life. This question of social convention versus naturalness will achieve paramount importance in the play's main plot, which asks whether a woman's natural role—not just her socially-expected role—is to serve her husband in a humble, acquiescent manner.

To complement this theme of social roles (or the "social order"), Shakespeare continues to point to the continued stagedness of the play itself. We have already mentioned the matter of boys playing the parts of women during the reigns of Elizabeth I and James I. We should also recall that the Lord particularly warns the players not to pay any attention to Sly should he "rave" and try to interrupt the play. With our modern notions of the stage, it is difficult for us to appreciate the self-consciousness of these instructions.

We should take into account, however, that the audience in an Elizabethan theater stood or sat very close to the stage, and even interacted with the players. The repartee between the noble Theseus and the players in *A Midsummer Night's Dream* is a good example of the kind of banter which could occur between audience and performer in Shakespeare's day. The fact that the Lord wishes to cut off this kind of interaction should alert us to the importance of the audience enjoying the spectacle for what it is, a staged performance or an act. This motif of voyeurism should remind us of the play's nagging question: how fundamentally different are men and women if mere change in costume permits us to confuse one for the other?

Study Questions

1. Where does the action take place?

2. Why do Christopher Sly and the hostess quarrel?

3. Is Sly a modest person?

4. Where is the Lord returning from when he finds Sly asleep?

5. What does the Lord decide to do with Sly?

6. Who arrives at the Lord's dwelling while he is making preparations?

7. What special instructions does the Lord give to the new arrivals?

8. How does the Lord plan to use his page?

9. What special instructions does the Lord send to his page?

10. Why does the Lord want to be present when Sly awakens?

Answers

1. The action takes place in England, in front of an alehouse and near a lord's home.

2. Sly has apparently broken some glasses in the alehouse, after drinking too much.

3. No. He tries to claim that his ancestors descended from France with William the Conqueror. Therefore, he at least had access to the aristocracy if not membership in it.

4. The Lord is returning from hunting.

5. The Lord plans to move Sly into his own home so that Sly will wake up to find himself dressed as a nobleman with servants.

6. A theatrical group comes to the Lord's house and asks to give a performance.

7. The Lord instructs the players to ignore any protests or signals from Sly. The Lord is afraid that Sly might not play along.

8. The Lord plans to dress up Bartholomew, his page, as the noble wife of Sly.

9. The Lord gives instructions that his page should use an onion to cry for joy should he not have a woman's gift to summon tears on command.

10. The Lord wants to be present to enjoy his joke on Sly, and to

make sure that his servants do not ruin the gag by laughing too much.

Suggested Essay Topics

1. Class differences are displayed in the opening scene of the Induction. Describe the differences between the Lord and Christopher Sly in regard to their behavior, speech, and their expectations of one another.

2. The differences between men and women are, illustrated by the fight between Sly and the Hostess, and referred to by the Lord's comment about a woman's ability to cry. Compare these two scenes and discuss how women and men are shown here to be similar and/or different. You will need to consider whether the claim that women can cry on command is true.

Induction, Scene 2

New Character:

Bartholomew: *the Lord's page who appears dressed as a woman ready to play Sly's wife*

Summary

Sly awakens and finds himself in bed, surrounded by servants who treat him as if he were nobility. The servants ask Sly, who is now in a fine gentleman's night apparel, whether he will have sack (wine) or other delectables. Sly protests that he is no gentleman, and that he has never drunk sack in his life. He recites a ridiculous personal history, but the servants pay him no attention.

According to the Lord's scheme, the servants remind Sly that this type of behavior is exactly what has kept his family away from his lordly estate and his wife from his bed. The Lord himself is present, dressed as a servant; he attempts to entice Sly, with sweet music and rich clothing, to think of himself as a sophisticated aristocrat. The Lord also suggests that Sly should ride about on his horse or go hunting and hawking. The servants then offer to bring

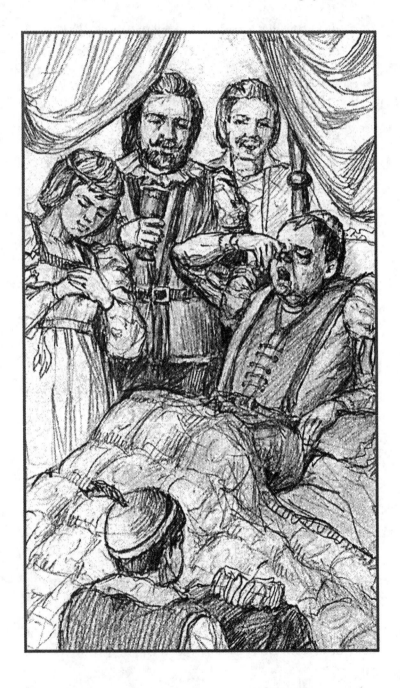

in fine paintings of mythological characters such as Venus (Cytherea), Adonis, and others.

The Lord finally addresses the matter of Sly's wife, who has supposedly been mourning his illness during his long "convalescence" (period of delusions). At this news, Sly perks up, renounces his identity as Christopher Sly the Tinker, and calls for his wife.

Bartholomew, the Lord's page, dressed as a woman, enters and inquires after Sly's health. Sly has some confusion over how to address a gentlewoman, but when this is cleared up, he orders the servants to depart and calls for his lady to join him in bed. Bartholomew, knowing that joining Sly in bed would reveal his true identity as a boy and end the elaborate joke, puts Sly off by mentioning that the doctor has forbidden marital relations lest Sly slip into his former delusions.

A messenger steps in to announce the entertainment arranged on Sly's behalf, "a pleasant comedy." Sly agrees to it, and the players file onto the stage below. (The action in this scene has taken place in a loft above the stage proper.)

Analysis

The second scene of the Induction continues to develop the themes of the initial scene. Class differences are asserted, and the question of natural inclination versus social convention is brought to the fore.

When Sly is treated as a nobleman, he is quick to renounce any such connection. Sly is aware that masquerading as a person of a higher station in society is unlawful and punishable by incarceration. Therefore, he rejects the fine clothes offered to him, and makes clear that he is used to owning only one pair of pants and socks and shoes at a time. His recitation of a family and personal history, however, does betray some pretention—note his awkward usage of "transmutation" and the significant mention of a "profession" rather than a vocation.

The servants play their parts according to the Lord's script. They are noticeably less articulate than the Lord himself, who goes on at length about the aristocratic pursuits of hunting, hawking, and riding horses. His speeches make reference to Apollo, Semiramis, and Io, while his servants follow suit by mentioning

Adonis, Cytherea, and Daphne—all mythological characters from Shakespeare's favorite classical work, Ovid's *Metamorphoses.*

These allusions (or references to other works of literature) help establish the Lord's own character as an educated and cultured person, since he obviously has read the writings to which he refers. It is significant that Sly does not respond to these allusions, for a person of his low station was probably illiterate.

In order to relate to Sly on his own level, the Lord shifts rhetorical gears by moving from the realm of high culture to the more mundane or perhaps the more natural—a man's appreciation for a woman. The Lord is quick to tell Sly that he has "a woman more beautiful/Than any woman in this waning age." This maneuver has the desired effect: Sly now accepts his new identity and calls his former life a mere dream.

Once the Page enters, however, two things go wrong to make Sly seem an idiot or worse. Sly does not even know how to address his wife, and Sly wants the crossdressed boy to come to bed. Ironically, the Page, who is after all just a boy (or perhaps a teenager) proves himself far more articulate than Sly. He uses a rhetorically sophisticated *chiasmus* in his speech— "My husband and my lord, my lord and husband." This classical device from oratory, of mirroring or repeating words, is intended to flatter the listener. Such polished speech is lost on Sly, who blunders by addressing his "lady" as "madam wife" rather than simply "madam." Sly shows his ignorance by forgetting his adroit servant's advice to call his lady "Madam, and nothing else."

Perhaps the greatest comic moment in the play comes when Sly calls for the Page to join him in bed. All the sexual tension suggested by one man embracing another comes to a climax here. It is completely lost on Sly, whose name is now ironically inappropriate since his actions and words have revealed him to be nothing short of a buffoon. Such moments of sexual tension occur repeatedly in Shakespeare's comedies. Indeed, it is hard to find a comedy in which this sort of mishap and misperception among characters does *not* occur. The final import of this scene may be variously interpreted, but we must be cognizant of the question which is raised here regarding the existence of supposedly natural inclinations—such as the attraction to the opposite sex. This scene asks the audience to compare Sly's response to Bartholomew dressed as a woman with Sly's presumed response to Bartholomew dressed as himself. The upshot of Sly's "mistake" is that he did not make a mistake at all; he merely made the choice his society required him to make—to choose a person in a woman's clothing for his bedfellow. Shakespeare leaves his audience to ponder, then, whether the *attraction* to the opposite sex (to say nothing of matters of procreation) is natural or conventional, that is, societally normalized and expected. To put the question another way: Are we attracted to clothes or to the person wearing them? Such a matter is no doubt difficult for us to consider, let alone to discuss, but we should keep in mind that social relations in Shakespeare's time were complex.

Study Questions

1. Where does Sly awaken?

2. How is Sly treated once he is awake?

3. How does Sly first respond to this treatment?

4. How does Sly describe himself?

5. What activities does the Lord suggest might be to Sly's liking?

6. What classical text do the Lord and his servants allude to when they mention mythological characters, such as Adonis and Io?

7. How does the Lord ultimately convince Sly that he is a lord and not just dreaming?

8. Describe Sly's reaction to his "wife."

9. Does Bartholomew join Sly in bed?

10. What sort of play is announced to Sly?

Answers

1. Sly awakens in a bedroom at the Lord's home.

2. The Lord's servants treat Sly as a gentleman, and offer him wine and rich clothing.

3. At first, Sly tries to renounce his new identity and all the ministrations of the Lord's servants.

4. Sly describes his ancestry, and his current vocation as a tinker (pot-mender), but does so in a pretentious way, as if he were a gentleman.

5. The Lord mentions riding, hunting, and hawking.

6. They refer to Ovid's *Metamorphoses*, a text alluded to in various ways in most of Shakespeare's works.

7. The Lord switches from talk of clothes and courtly activities, of which Sly is ignorant, to mention of Sly's beautiful wife.

8. Sly is instantly attracted to Bartholomew dressed up as a woman.

9. No. Bartholomew cannot join Sly because that would lead to Sly finding out that his "wife" is nothing but a cross-dressed boy, and reveal the joke the Lord has played on him.

10. The play is at first described as a comedy, but on further questioning Bartholomew calls it a kind of history. The first description is accurate.

Suggested Essay Topics

1. Explain Sly's change of heart to accept his new identity as a gentleman. What has brought this change about? What was his attitude toward being a gentleman before and after this turnaround?

2. Describe the sexual tension when Sly asks for his wife to join him in bed. Why must Bartholomew refuse Sly?

3. Consider how Shakespeare forces his audience to speculate about the naturalness of a person's attraction to the opposite sex. How does Shakespeare suggest that this attraction might actually be conventional (that is, socially patterned) as well as (or instead of) naturally inclined?

Act I

Act I, Scene 1

New Characters:

Katharina: *the shrew who rejects suitors*

Bianca: *Katharina's beautiful younger sister who cannot marry until a man weds Katharina*

Lucentio: *a young man who wants to marry Bianca*

Baptista: *the wealthy father of Katharina and Bianca*

Gremio and **Hortensio:** *suitors to Bianca*

Tranio: *Lucentio's servant who disguises himself as his master*

Biondello: *young servant to Lucentio*

Summary

Lucentio, a wealthy young man, arrives in Padua, a city famous in Shakespeare's time for its university. He has come with his servant, Tranio, from Pisa, supposedly renowned for its "grave citizens." Lucentio mentions that his father is a merchant, and that he himself has been raised in Florence, the urban jewel of Italian culture. His father has made his fortune in business, technically making him a member of the *bourgeoisie* the merchant middle class, not the aristocracy. Lucentio has come to Padua to study philosophy, but Tranio warns him that "No profit grows where is no pleasure ta'en," meaning that he should enjoy himself while at

the university. Tranio even reminds his master not to forget Ovid, the poet who wrote the *Metamorphoses*, to which Shakespeare alludes throughout this play.

The conversation between master and servant is interrupted by an exchange of noisy words. Baptista is the father of Katharina (the shrew) and Bianca. Gremio and Hortensio want to marry the fair, younger daughter Bianca, but are rebuffed by Baptista, who stipulates that the elder sister, Katharina, must be married before he will give away Bianca. Katharina protests to her father that he is unnecessarily submitting her to ridicule by not marrying off Bianca and by talking in public with suitors who curse her. Gremio and Hortenio do in fact heap insults upon Katharina, and she answers them in kind.

Hortensio reminds Baptista that it is unfair to Bianca to keep her locked away at home with Katharina while so many men seek her hand in marriage. Baptista responds that if he does not insist that Katharina be married first, he will never be able to give her away. In the meantime, Baptista suggests, he will take in "cunning men" to educate his daughters in the liberal arts (e.g., music and poetry).

Once Baptista and his daughters leave, Hortensio shares with Gremio a scheme he has just devised. Hortensio asks for Gremio's help to find a man to marry Katharina so that they will then have access to Bianca. Gremio doubts that such a plan will work. No man would want to marry this sharp-tongued woman he likens to "hell." Hortensio reminds Gremio that Baptista is very wealthy, and that some man will take Katharina solely for her dowry. Gremio accedes to the plan.

Tranio notices that Lucentio has been staring after Bianca as if he has fallen in love on first sight. Lucentio admits as much. He tries to compare himself to the Queen of Carthage, Dido, the most famous tragic victim of Virgil's great epic, *The Aeneid*—another classical text to which Shakespeare often alludes. Lucentio blunders the comparison by relating himself instead to Dido's sister, Anna.

Tranio ignores the tragic implications of the comparison (Dido committed suicide), and warns his master to ransom himself from the imprisonment of love. The servant points toward a stumbling block in Lucentio's presumed courtship of Bianca, but Lucentio apparently has not been paying attention to what has transpired between the father and the suitors. Tranio must explain that the elder daughter must be married first, before Bianca, and that there is hardly any chance for that to happen.

Lucentio comes to his senses, and reminds Tranio that the father will accept "cunning schoolmasters." Tranio sees his point. He suggests that Lucentio enter Baptista's home, disguised as a schoolmaster, and woo Bianca. But Lucentio enjoins Tranio to cover for him while he tutors Bianca. Tranio accepts his mission to disguise himself as his master. The two switch clothes.

Biondello, another servant of Lucentio, enters and becomes confused by the new appearance of the two men. Lucentio deceives Biondello about his motivation for changing identities by claiming that he has killed a man and must now escape without being recognized. Biondello does not believe his master, but goes along with his instructions to treat Tranio as a gentleman in public and to call him Lucentio.

Above the stage, up in a loft, servants to Christopher Sly rouse Sly out of his sleep and tell him that he has not been paying attention to the play. Sly asks how much is left to be performed. When he finds out that it has only just begun, he exclaims that he wishes it were done.

Analysis

In many of his plays, Shakespeare depicts a young man falling instantly in love with a girl he sees for the first time. The device usually allows the playwright to show some of the failings that occur in love due to naïveté. However in this comedy, Shakespeare does not engage the youth in ridiculous situations. Instead, he keeps the action light-hearted and amusing. For instance, once Lucentio sees Bianca, who appears to him as beautiful as her fair name—white—suggests, he seems to go into a trance, from which Tranio must awaken him.

The playwright also foreshadows the festive nature of this comedy by having Tranio remind Lucentio that his studies must not be too severe. Tranio even drops two important names to underscore his point:

Let's be no stoics nor no stocks, I pray,
Or so devote to Aristotle's checks
As Ovid be an outcast quite abjur'd. (I.i.31-33)

Aristotle was known throughout the Medieval period and into the Renaissance as the writer of mysterious philosophical treatises, such as *The Metaphysics*, in which he mandates strict social roles for men and women. Further, his *Poetics* dictated strict rules to keep tragedy separate from comedy, rules which were both championed and contested from the Renaissance to the eighteenth century.

Ovid, on the other hand, was brazenly comic,though sophisticated, Latin love poet who, more often than not, mixed tragedy with burlesque humor by subjecting the male lover to the slavery of a female beloved. This was especially true in his *Amores* and *The Art of Love*, both of which Shakespeare relies upon thematically to complicate the sexual relations in his plays. With the mentioning of Ovid, then, the playwright prepares the audience to expect to see men enslaving themselves to their mistresses. By having Tranio prefer Ovid to Aristotle, Shakespeare indicates that this play will not follow traditional rules of decorum, and that it is intended to give pleasure and educate.

Shakespeare also wishes to create the impression that Lucentio is far from home. We learn from his speech that he has come from Pisa, which is a considerable distance from Padua. Shakespeare could easily have set this play in Bologna, another famous university town much closer to Pisa. But the playwright wants the audience to think that the young man is far from home and free, as Lucentio hopes, from the control of his father—though this will later turn out to be an incorrect assumption.

The fighting between Katharina and her father, her suitors, and later her husband, Petruchio, has been vigorously contested by critics. With the rise of feminism in the twentieth century, many readers now see Katharina as a victim of a male-dominated culture. Others claim that Katharina deserves the insults hurled at her because she is unwilling to give a man his due and to submit herself to a husband's demands. No doubt, a position exists which combines these two views.

An audience's appraisal of this situation will be shaped by the performance, particularly the portrayal of Katharina. The reader, in contrast, has only the text to judge by, and from the text it is clear that Katharina appears in a defensive posture, responding to the nasty remarks which Gremio makes to her. Further inspection reveals that Katharina does have a reputation; judging from the cleverness with which she verbally outmatches Gremio and later Hortensio, she seems to have earned her reputation as a shrew.

The men in this scene are not saints, however. There is ample evidence to suggest that Gremio, Hortensio, and even Katharina's father, Baptista, have purely selfish motives in this quarrel. Baptista obviously does not wish to live alone with his feisty daughter, and he is willing to use Bianca as leverage in order to get rid of Katharina. Gremio and Hortensio do not see Katharina as a person, but merely as a stumbling block to their own courtship of Bianca.

Lucentio, though removed from the verbal fight with Katharina, implicates himself as a scoundrel by referring to Bianca as the "daughter of Agenor...That made great Jove to humble him to her hand,/When with his knees he kiss'd the Cretan strand" (I.i.168-70). The allusion is again to Ovid's *Metamorphoses*. At the end of Book Two, Jupiter changes himself into a bull to beguile the lovely Europa, whom he carries across the sea to Crete and then rapes. While Lucentio makes the image sound pretty, it carries monstrous overtones. His allusion also foreshadows his own scheme to change his appearance in order to gain access to Bianca's quarters, where he intends to woo her.

Lucentio's plan to switch roles with his servant should remind the reader of the Lord's role-switching with Sly in the Induction. Indeed, the playwright signals our attention to Sly's presence above the stage, for we may have forgotten about him in the same way that he has fallen asleep and does not "mind the play." The fact that Lucentio and Tranio are interchangeable in the eyes of the citizens of Padua suggests that there is nothing innately superior about either of these men. This theme also parallels the question suggested by the cross-dressing motif introduced when Bartholomew successfully masquerades as a woman.

Study Questions

1. Under what special circumstances does Act One begin?

2. Where do Lucentio and Tranio arrive in the first scene, and why have they come to this town?

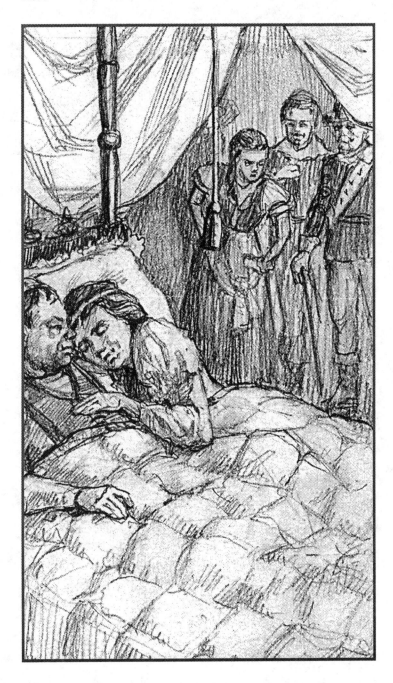

3. Whom do Lucentio and Tranio witness quarreling?

4. Why will Baptista not give away Bianca at present?

5. How does Katharina treat the suitors of Bianca?

6. What scheme does Hortensio concoct in order to marry Bianca?

7. With whom has Lucentio fallen in love?

8. How does Lucentio intend to woo Bianca?

9. What is Tranio's role in Lucentio's plan?

10. How does Sly like the play so far?

Answers

1. Act One begins with Sly and his "wife" sitting above the stage in a loft, so as to view the play the Lord has prepared as entertainment for Sly.

2. They arrive in Padua, a city famous for its university. Lucentio has come to study philosophy.

3. They see two suitors, Gremio and Hortensio, speaking with Baptista and Katharina. Bianca speaks only four lines.

4. Baptista knows that if he does not marry off Katharina before Bianca, he will have to spend the rest of his days listening to her sharp tongue. He uses Bianca as leverage to send away Katharina as soon as possible.

5. Katharina returns the insults of Gremio and Hortensio, and goads them.

6. Hortensio enlists Gremio to find a suitable man to marry Katharina, despite Gremio's disbelief that such a man exists. Hortensio thinks that some man, desiring her rich dowry, will marry her.

7. Lucentio has fallen in love at first sight with Bianca; he has hardly noticed Katharina.

8. Lucentio plans to dress himself as a schoolmaster in order to be introduced into Bianca's presence, where he intends to make covert overtures for her affection.

9. Lucentio asks Tranio to dress as his master so that the people of the town will still know that Lucentio has arrived.

10. Sly probably does not appreciate the play, for he has fallen asleep. Servants have roused him so that he will watch the rest.

Suggested Essay Topics

1. Many critics question whether Katharina deserves her reputation as a shrew. Compare the remarks made by Gremio, "shrew," a "fiend of hell" and so on.

2. Bianca utters a mere four lines in this scene (ll. 80-83). Characterize the import of her words here, and compare her attitude with that of her older sister.

3. Biondello immediately recognizes his master despite the disguise. But Lucentio thinks that the citizens of Padua will take him for a schoolmaster and Tranio for a merchant's son if they simply dress up as those persons. How does this kind of role-switching compare with that of the gendered role reversal performed by the page in the Induction? How would each instance of role change be tolerated in modern society?

Act I, Scene 2

New Characters:

Petruchio—*a forceful man who intends to marry for money*

Grumio—*Petruchio's patient servant*

Summary

Petruchio arrives in Padua from his hometown of Verona. His father, Antonio, has just died. Petruchio plans to take a wife in Padua and to visit his old friends. In front of the home of his friend Hortensio, Petruchio orders the elderly servant Grumio to knock on the door for him. But Grumio misunderstands, and a scuffle ensues. The clamor brings out Hortensio, who recognizes his old friend and invites the pair in.

Having heard Petruchio's plan "to wive and thrive" wealthily in Padua, Hortensio mentions Baptista's daughter Katharina. He entices Petruchio with her rich dowry. Petruchio takes immediate interest in Katharina's dowry and puts off any talk of being afraid of her sharp tongue. Petruchio reminds Hortensio of the weight of gold on one's preferences. Grumio, speaking from experience, gives Petruchio a vote of confidence.

Hortensio then divulges his plan to woo Bianca covertly, as a schoolmaster of music. At this moment, Gremio enters with Lucentio dressed as a schoolmaster. Gremio instructs Lucentio privately to speak to Bianca on his behalf, and to read only the books of love poetry which are on the list he then gives to Lucentio. Lucentio promises to plead to Bianca in private on Gremio's behalf.

Hortensio tries to interrupt the pair, and Gremio reveals to Hortensio only that he intends to provide schooling in poetry to Bianca. Hortensio explains their good fortune in finding Petruchio to marry Kate so that they may both court Bianca. Gremio dismisses the match, but Petruchio assures him that if he has been able to withstand fierce battles and raging seas, he can easily tolerate one woman's mouth. Hortensio enlists Gremio's aid to pull off the match.

Tranio, dressed as Lucentio, enters with Biondello as his servant. When Tranio asks for directions to Baptista Minola's home, the other men become worried that he intends to court the object of their affections. Tranio declares his wish to court Bianca. He calms the passions of Gremio and Hortensio by reminding them that the right man will always win his bride.

Once the men establish that Tranio seeks the younger daughter, whom he has never seen, Hortensio reveals their conspiracy to help Petruchio marry Kate first so that they will all have access to Bianca. Tranio agrees to the conspiracy, and Hortensio offers to introduce Petruchio to Baptista.

Analysis

This scene establishes the characters of the men who will set the terms for courting the two sisters, Katharina and Bianca. Petruchio will court Kate openly, and the other men will resort to surreptitious means to gain access to Bianca. The fact that they

must rely on Petruchio to clear the way to Bianca only reinforces the idea that these men cannot court a woman on their own or by "honest" means. Gremio, Hortensio, and Lucentio have each plotted a way to woo Bianca in secret, out of the reach of the restrictive father, Baptista. To what extent dressing up as a schoolmaster demeans a man of wealth such as Lucentio remains a question.

Petruchio comes to Padua partly to visit with his friends but mostly to find a wealthy wife. He is quite honest about his intentions to marry a woman for her money. When Hortensio cautions Petruchio about Katharina's ability to scold, Petruchio chastizes him that he has forgotten "gold's effect," that is, the way money can entice one to forget shortcomings and to see only the pleasure it can buy. Petruchio even lists several women, famous for their lack of beauty, who would be tolerable given the right incentive. One woman, Florentius' wife, is not even named, so trivial is she. She was well-known, nonetheless, to readers in Shakespeare's time as the lady who is transformed into a beautiful woman in Chaucer's *The Wife of Bath's Tale* and also in Gower's *Confessio Amantis*. This allusion foreshadows Katharina's own transformation at the end of the play.

Hortensio's disingenuousness is remarkably evident in this scene. Hortensio claims to have mentioned Katharina as a jest, but Petruchio's offer to marry her is clearly a dream come true. The other suitors, Gremio and Tranio (who pretends to be Lucentio), are similarly overjoyed at the offer, and they agree to help speed Petruchio's courtship of Kate in any way they can. This conspiracy sets the stage for the abduction, rather than the courtship, of Kate.

Grumio, Petruchio's servant, has real faith in Petruchio's ability to marry "Katharine the curst." This epithet may in fact be a reminder of Henry VIII's first wife, Catharine "the First" (there has been no second), who bitterly opposed the monarch's plan to reform the Church by replacing the Catholic Church with the Church of England. Grumio claims that Petruchio will "rail in his rope-tricks...he will throw a figure in her face and so disfigure her with it that she shall have no more eyes to see withal than a cat." His words, though difficult to construe at first, actually foreshadow the play's action. Grumio envisions Petruchio tying up Katharina so that she will have to do what he says, while he flashes verbal tricks in her face. In other words, Grumio knows Petruchio to be a rhetorical genius.

There was evidence of such verbal virtuosity at the scene's opening. When Petruchio asks, "Knock me here soundly," he intends that Grumio should knock for him on Hortensio's door. Grumio takes Petruchio literally to mean "Knock here on my head hard," which a servant should never do to his master. To Grumio, this playing with the literalness and figurativeness of words makes Petruchio an excellent verbal craftsman. While Grumio is perhaps not too believable, he is credible on this point.

Petruchio announces that he knows how to court a woman properly, especially a shrew. He does not mean to woo her in the traditional sense. Instead, he plans an assault: "I will board her, though she chide as loud/As thunder when the clouds in autumn crack." The literal sense here is sexually vulgar, and it may be intended; but the figurative sense of boarding, as in boarding a ship, is also suggestive of the way he means to capture Katharina. He will not wait to be invited. He must seize the day by seizing the woman.

Ignoring Gremio's pessimism that "such a life with such a wife were strange," Petruchio boasts that he has done things far more difficult, and manly, than taming a shrew. Displaying some of his rhetorical genius for the first time, Petruchio spontaneously composes a speech to insist that Katharina will be easy prey for him: "Have I not in a pitched battle heard/Loud 'larums, neighing steeds, and trumpets' clang?/And do you tell me of a woman's tongue...?" Finally, Petruchio puts aside rhetoric altogether: "To what end are all these words?" Petruchio clearly means to take Katharina by force, not by guile or verbal persuasion.

Study Questions

1. Why has Petruchio come to Padua?

2. Why does Petruchio box Grumio's ears?

3. Whose house does Petruchio enter?

4. What does Hortensio suggest to Petruchio?

5. With whom does Gremio conspire to achieve Bianca?

6. What is Gremio's attitude toward Petruchio's attempt to marry Kate?

7. What does Grumio mean when he says that Petruchio will disfigure Kate so that she will not be able to see?

8. Why does Tranio appear at Hortensio's home?

9. What is Lucentio doing in the meantime?

10. Why does Tranio go along with the men's scheme?

Answers

1. Petruchio arrives in Padua partly to visit friends but mainly to find a wealthy wife.

2. Grumio incurs Petruchio's wrath when he does not knock on the door for him as a servant should for his master.

3. Petruchio enters Hortensio's home.

4. Hortensio mentions the wealthy dowry of Katharina, and suggests that Petruchio try to marry her.

5. Gremio arranges for Lucentio, now disguised as a school-master, to woo Bianca for him while reading selected works of love poetry to her.

6. Gremio does not believe anyone can find a fit mate in Katharina, but he will be pleased if Petruchio marries her.

7. Grumio seems to have picked up Petruchio's knack for figurative language here. He means that Kate will be so blinded by Petruchio's rhetoric that she will readily give her hand in marriage and submit to his every whim.

8. Tranio comes dressed as Lucentio to ask directions to Baptista's home.

9. Lucentio, who has just agreed to woo Bianca on Gremio's behalf, keeps out of the way and listens to the conversation.

10. Tranio has nothing at stake here. He must simply help his master to marry Bianca, and Tranio realizes that Katharina must be wedded first.

Suggested Essay Topics

1. Only Petruchio plans to woo a woman openly while Gremio, Hortensio and Lucentio contrive schemes to gain access to Bianca. Compare the plans of each suitor and decide whose is the most clever and whose the most "manly." Explain your reasoning.

2. Petruchio appears in this scene as a rough man. Describe why this is so by examining his words and his actions around the other men.

3. Master and servant quarrel at the beginning of this scene over a small linguistic misunderstanding. Explain the nature of this mishap first. Then calculate whether Grumio really misunderstands Petruchio. Base your answer on evidence provided by Grumio's asides to the audience during this scene.

Act II

Act II, Scene 1

Summary

At Baptista's home, Katharina interrogates Bianca, whose hands are bound. The elder sister wants to know which suitor Bianca prefers, but the younger sister will not admit to favoring either Hortensio or the rich Gremio. Bianca offers to stay away from the man of Katharina's choice, but perceives that Kate has been jesting. This idea inflames Kate, who then strikes Bianca.

Baptista enters and interposes himself between the two sisters. Bianca runs out after Kate attempts to strike her a second time. Kate once again charges her father with trying to humiliate her.

The old and new suitors arrive. Petruchio presents Hortensio as Litio, a musician. Gremio presents Lucentio, disguised as Cambio, a schoolmaster. Tranio announces himself as Lucentio, and gives Baptista books and a lute.

Petruchio hastily asks to be permitted to court Kate immediately. The father quickly settles the terms of her dowry first: Baptista offers one half of his lands upon his death and 20,000 crowns up front; Petruchio grants Kate all his lands and leases in the event that she should survive him. When Baptista suggests that wooing Kate will be a difficult affair, Petruchio reassures him that he can aptly persuade a woman of Kate's nature.

Hortensio enters with his lute broken over his head and dangling around his neck. When asked what has happened, Hortensio claims that Katharina would prove a better soldier than

wife. The report of Kate's behavior excites Petruchio, who declares that he wishes to speak with her now more than ever. The two men leave, and Petruchio soliloquizes about the technique of courtship he will employ to woo Kate; he intends to flatter her.

Kate comes in. Petruchio greets her politely, but Kate treats him rudely and dismissively. A verbal sparring match ensues wherein Kate rejects Petruchio repeatedly while Petruchio continues to flatter and to taunt Kate using sexual innuendos. Kate strikes him, but Petruchio ends their conversation by claiming that he intends to marry her, that he will not be refused, and that the marriage has already been agreed to by her father.

Baptista, Gremio, and Tranio enter conveniently at this point and ask how Petruchio has fared. Petruchio feigns success. He must save face by claiming that Kate and he fight in the presence of others but act mildly when alone. The men quickly congratulate him on his progress.

Tranio tries to assert his claim to Bianca by needling Gremio about his old age. Gremio fires back that he probably has more material possessions to offer than Tranio. Baptista interrupts them at this sensitive moment by asking how each suitor will provide for his daughter. Gremio promises his house and all his furnishings upon his death. Tranio proffers all his lands and houses. Moreover, Tranio suggests that because of his youth, he will not leave Bianca a lonely widow, as Gremio will surely do on account of his old age. As Tranio's offer far and away exceeds that of Gremio, Baptista decides to let Tranio court Bianca.

Analysis

The reader will notice that this scene comprises the entire act. Not only is the length of the act appropriate for comedy, but the fact that there is no change of venue necessitates the action being enclosed in a single scene. The staging of one long act with no change of scenery permits the action to take place rapidly. The quick pace reflects the flimflam style behind Petruchio's courtship of Kate.

When the act begins, Kate seems to have let paranoia get the best of her. But the audience may change its mind when Katharina reminds Bianca that Gremio is old and rich. This thought might appear callous, but Katharina would not be alone here. Her father,

Baptista, for example, is interested most in the financial security of his children, though he claims, disingenuously, that Kate's love "is all in all" (129).

Petruchio seems even more hard-hearted than Baptista, for he dismisses outright Kate's preferences. He claims simply that he is "peremptory" (131) and will not be turned down. When questioned again how he will tame a fiery mate, Petruchio says that "where two raging fires meet together/They do consume the thing that feeds their fury" (132-33). In other words, the pair might seem incompatible because the individuals are too similar. Not so, says Petruchio. Only like-minded mates can compete with each other, and quell their fury, he says.

Petruchio accurately assesses his courtship style as peremptory. In his soliloquy, lines 169-81, he lets the audience in on the most persuasive element of his "wooing dance," which is flattery. At this point, Petruchio assumes an identity in the play which had only been suggested heretofore by his name; he now becomes a *Petrarchan lover.* Renaissance audiences were attuned to sophisticated verbal play in English, French, or Italian, which came to London via traders and theater companies. So the sound of Petruchio's name would subliminally register the famous Italian love poet, Francesco Petrarca—in English, Petrarch. It is also fair to think that Petruchio's name would call to mind the French word *perruque* (wig) and the Italian verb *truccare* (to cheat), which in its reflexive form signifies the act of putting on make-up. All these hints are underlined by Petruchio's behavior in this scene and elsewhere.

The importance of Petrarchan love poetry to Shakespeare's works cannot be ignored. For our purposes here, however, we need simply be aware that Shakespeare used and alluded to Petrarch's poetic style in three basic ways: first, in order to show how a lover might speak and act while in love; second, to make fun of that lover when his behavior is too excessive; and third, to show how an experienced lover handles his affairs. Two of Shakespeare's sonnets, composed probably slightly later than *The Taming of the Shrew,* demonstrate the first and third attitudes just mentioned. The sonnets themselves document the course of one lover's journey from a youthful to a more sophisticated, if not cynical, view of love. Sonnet 26 captures the spirit of a simple lover who cowers before his beloved, in this case another man:

Lord of my love, to whom in vassalage
Thy merit hath my duty strongly knit,
To thee I send this written embassage
To witness duty, not to show my wit;
Duty so great which wit so poor as mine
May make seem bare in wanting words to show it,
But that I hope some good conceit of thine
In thy soul's thought, all naked, will bestow it,
Till whatsoever star that guides my moving
Points on me graciously with fair aspect,
And puts apparel on my tattered loving
To show me worthy of thy sweet respect.
 Then may I dare to boast how I do love thee;
 Till then, not show my head where thou mayst prove me.

Here the lover obsequiously implores the beloved to accept
his supposedly unrefined poetry.

Sonnet 138, in contrast, portrays an older, wiser lover, like
Petruchio. He is content to flatter his beloved, here a woman, and
be flattered likewise:

When my love swears that she is made of truth
I do believe her though I know she lies,
That she might think me some untutored youth
Unlearned in the world's false subtleties.
Thus vainly thinking that she thinks me young,
Although she knows my days are past the best,
Simply I credit her false-speaking tongue;
On both sides thus is simple truth suppressed.
But wherefore says she not she is unjust,
And wherefore say not I that I am old?
O, love's best habit is in seeming trust,
And age in love loves not to have years told.
 Therefore I lie with her, and she with me,
 And in our faults by lies we flattered be.

Though this sonnet refers mostly to the technique of flattery
used by the beloved on the lover, this approach is clearly the one
used by Petruchio in order to woo Kate. This variety of to love is
not the overly serious and unsophisticated sort practiced by young,
"novice" lovers, as Petruchio calls Tranio and Hortensio (308). A

perruqued and tricky Petrarchan lover, on the other hand, would masquerade in flattery.

Petruchio's soliloquy emphasizes the idea that he must force himself to be kind to a mean-spirited Kate. Petruchio must reinterpret her puns, which paint him in a negative light, and transform them into sexually suggestive comments. Petruchio's success in verbal combat irritates Kate to the point of striking him. Petruchio promises to bind her if she continue. He then begins to flatter Kate, but he also compares her to Diana, the goddess of the hunt. The comparison is ambivalent, for Diana was not only regarded as beautiful, she was also fiercely independent. For example, as Ovid's story in the *Metamorphoses* has it, Diana turned the young man Actaeon into a stag to be torn apart by his own dogs after he observed her bathing.

When Baptista and the other suitors reappear, Petruchio changes the comparison to "Grissel/And Roman Lucrece" (292-93). The strategy again is to flatter Kate; Grisselda and Lucrece were famous for patience and chastity, respectively, these qualities being womanly virtues during the Renaissance. Boccaccio had written in Italian of Grisselda in his *Decameron*. Petrarch translated the story into Latin, so that it would be more accessible to other Europeans. Not long after, Chaucer wrote his own version of the Grisselda story in the Clerk's Tale, part of his *Canterbury Tales*. The comparison to Lucrece foreshadows an event in the play's final scene that concerns a bet as to a woman's obedience. This substitutes here for a woman's chastity, which is Lucrece's claim to fame. The original story comes from the Roman historian Livy, but is retold time and again by writers such as Augustine, Petrarch and, not surprisingly, Shakespeare in his *Rape of Lucrece*, composed about the time *The Taming of the Shrew* appeared on stage. Petrarch, interestingly enough, was more concerned with the story of Brutus, Lucrece's husband, in his *De viris illustribus* (On Famous Men). We will have occasion to unravel the full complexity of the comparison in the final scene. For now, the reader should note that the comparison of Kate to Lucrece points also to the way Petruchio resembles Brutus, who became famous for cleverly playing the part of an idiot. Thus the comparison flatters both Kate as virtuous and Petruchio himself as clever.

The well-performed acting, both by Petruchio and by Baptista, is not lost on Kate. She chastises her father for "think[ing] with oaths to *face* the matter out" (286) in his "tender fatherly *regard*" (283). Here, Katharina plays upon the sense of *faces* as false appearances, which may be used to smooth things over so that her father may be rid of her quietly. Once Petruchio and Kate have departed, Baptista admits that he has played "a merchant's part" (323), as if selling his daughters. Even Tranio reveals his capitalistic spirit by objectifying Bianca as a "commodity" (325), which must be traded for profit.

The scene ends with a soliloquy from Tranio. He reminds the audience that he must have a father's blessing before Baptista will give away his daughter. Tranio also refers to himself as the "suppos'd" Lucentio and to "his" father as the "suppos'd" Vincentio. Shakespeare alludes here to the English play, *Supposes*, from which he took the Lucentio-Bianca subplot. Knowing that his audience would be familiar with this play, which was performed ten years earlier in London, Shakespeare makes reference to a bastard child (408), which has nothing to do with the current plot as he has reshaped it. In the original play, however, Bianca's analogue conceives out of wedlock and is forced to marry. With the last line, which puns on "child" in the double sense of baby and bastard, Shakespeare winks at a sophisticated Elizabethan audience which would have been familiar with the source of the play's plot. The reference is lost on a modern audience that has not seen Gascoigne's play.

Study Questions

1. What color is Kate's hair?

2. Why has Kate bound Bianca's hands?

3. Who offers Baptista gifts?

4. Why do the men believe that Petruchio has successfully wooed Kate when she rejects him publicly?

5. How does Baptista resolve the strife between Gremio and Tranio, who both seek the hand of Bianca?

6. What does Gremio offer to give Bianca?

7. How does Tranio's offer compare to Gremio's?

8. When are Katharina and Bianca to be married?

9. How does Gremio react to Baptista favoring Tranio's offer?

10. What does Tranio mean when he says that a "child shall get a sire"(408)?

Answers

1. She is probably a brunette, as Petruchio refers to her as a hazel-twig, and brown in hue.

2. She is interrogating Bianca about which suitor she prefers.

3. Strictly speaking, only Tranio does. He presents Baptista with a lute and some books. Both Petruchio and Gremio offer the services of teachers.

4. Petruchio has invented a clever story. The couple will be mean in public and mild in private. The men have a conflict of interest and are bound to believe Petruchio's story.

5. Baptista will choose the suitor who is best able to provide for his daughter.

6. Gremio can only offer his land and what little he has in his house, so he takes pains to enumerate all his minor possessions.

7. Tranio's offer far surpasses Gremio's. Tranio could give many properties and their rents to Bianca if she outlives her husband.

8. Katharina and Petruchio will marry on the upcoming Sunday, while Bianca and presumably Tranio will be married on the following Sunday, one week later.

9. Gremio suffers from sour grapes. He implies that Bianca is not worth all the money that Tranio has promised her, and that Tranio's father was a fool to have entrusted so much wealth to his son.

10. On the one hand, he refers to himself as a child, a young man, who must find an old man to play the part of father for "his" upcoming marriage. On the other hand, this line suggests the age-old problem of conception out of wedlock and a man forced to marry.

Suggested Essay Topics

1. Describe Petruchio's courtship of Kate. What methods does he use? Is he successful?

2. Compare the suitors' dowry offers. Why does Baptista accept Tranio's offer over Gremio's? How does this compare to Petruchio's promise?

3. Examine Kate's behavior in this scene. Why does she treat people in such a harsh manner?

Act III

Act III, Scenes 1 and 2

Summary

In Baptista's home, the two disguised suitors, Lucentio and Hortensio, compete for Bianca's attention. Lucentio asks Hortensio to go away to tune his instrument, and Bianca seconds him.

Lucentio reads an excerpt from Ovid's *Heroides* to Bianca. He tells her, in between lines of Latin poetry and in place of a translation, that he intends to court her. Bianca plays coy and does not reject Lucentio outright.

Hortensio returns and Bianca sends him off again, saying that his treble strings jar the harmony. Hortensio returns shortly, and hands Bianca a love note, hastily encoded in musical terminology, which she reads but rejects.

A servant interrupts the lessons to tell Bianca to go to her elder sister, who must prepare for the upcoming wedding. Bianca excuses herself from her "lessons" and departs, leaving Lucentio with Hortensio. Lucentio exits immediately, and Hortensio soliloquizes that Bianca has cast too loving a glance upon the schoolmaster. Hortensio becomes indignant that she could fall for such a common man as he seems, and decides not to pursue his courtship of Bianca.

Act III, Scene ii begins on Katharina's wedding day. When Petruchio has not yet arrived, Baptista laments that he and his daughter will be stood up. Katharina is understandly distraught as well. Tranio tries to console and reassure them, but Katharina departs.

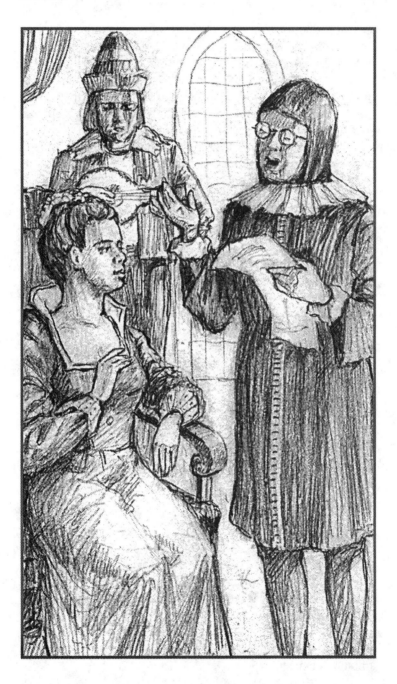

Biondello announces that he sees Petruchio coming—dressed in old attire and mounted on a broken and sick horse. After some buffoonery between the servant and Baptista, Petruchio finally arrives. Both Baptista and Tranio ridicule Petruchio for coming to his own wedding dressed as a common vagrant, and they advise him to change clothing immediately. Petruchio spurns them and goes off in search of a kiss from his bride.

Tranio reassures Lucentio in private that they will be able to find an old man to assume the role of his father, Vicentio.

Gremio comes out to tell what has occurred during the wedding service. He calls Petruchio a devil, compared to whom Kate seems a lamb. Gremio also reports that Petruchio struck the priest during the service, and gave Katharina a kiss which pealed loudly through the church.

Petruchio and the wedding entourage appear from the church. The groom declares that he must leave Padua immediately. All entreat him to stay, but he refuses. Even Katharina cannot entice Petruchio to attend his own wedding banquet. She finally becomes irascible, saying that she will stay in Padua even if he leaves. This challenge to his domestic authority fires Petruchio into a rage, and he proceeds to harangue Kate and the rest about a wife's duty to obey her husband. He also maintains that wives are the property of the heads of household.

Having finished his speech, Petruchio intimates that the other men want to steal his Katharine away from him. He then draws his sword, grabs Kate, and departs with his servant, Grumio. The rest marvel. Baptista asks the guests to take their places at the table and to enjoy the banquet.

Analysis

Act III, Scene i is a short scene which breaks up the long course of the last act, which is comprised of only one scene. Unlike the previous scene's competitive verbal combat, this scene pits two lovers against one another for comic effect. Both lovers appear somewhat ridiculous as they try to make their intentions known to Bianca, who is hardly caught off guard by their disguises. The beloved here shows herself more in control than either suitor. She asserts her will by dismissing Hortensio and checking the ambition of Lucentio.

The reader may wonder why Shakespeare has chosen to include lines from Ovid's *Heroides* (Heroines) rather than from the more popular *Metamorphoses, The Art of Love,* or *Amores* (Love Affairs). The *Heroides* was more popular in Chaucer's day, as his numerous references to the work reflect. The lines here are from Penelope's letter to Ulysses, the first epistle in Ovid's collection. Penelope reports a description of Troy, a place she of course has never seen, for she is still at home in Ithaca awaiting the return of her husband. Perhaps there is a far-off allusion to Helen, the face, as Marlowe puts it in *Dr. Faustus,* that "launched a thousand ships." If not, then presumably Shakespeare refers to Ovid's heroines in order to emphasize through association Bianca's strength of character and craftiness.

Bianca rejects Hortensio's overture hastily, though it seems arranged no more sloppily than Lucentio's. Bianca, therefore, appears capricious. Hortensio's comments in soliloquy to underscore this point, though clearly his perception of Bianca is conflicted by his interest in her.

In Act III, Scene ii, Petruchio employs a new strategy in his attempt to tame his shrewish wife. Before he had flattered Kate, but now he humiliates her by arriving late to his own wedding and coming underdressed and ill-equipped. Baptista accuses Petruchio of dressing below his station, and shaming both himself and Baptista's honor. To answer his accusation, Petruchio quickly invents a reason for his deportment, stating emphatically, "To me she's married not unto my clothes" (116). The line ironically reminds the audience that everyone on the stage is an actor.

Later, this theatrical motif recurs when Petruchio declares that Katherina is "my house,/My household stuff, my *field,* my *barn,*/My horse, my ox, my ass, my any thing" (229-31). At first glance, these lines seem hyperbolically patriarchal and chauvinistic, yet a savvy reader will notice the allusions to the ribald poet Richard Barnfield, who wrote love poetry about male-male sexual encounters among the English nobility. A crossdressed boy, performs the part of Kate and the modern reader may well have guessed what historical research has found to be true about Elizabethan male sexuality—boys were taken for sexual objects by adult men. If such a fact is astonishing, one has only to recall a similar practice among the ancient Greeks.

Tranio, who is of course disguised as Lucentio, acknowledges the effectiveness of Petruchio's dressing down when he confesses, "He has some meaning in his mad attire" (123).

The reader will notice the *chiasmus* used in Gremio's speech for comic effect (163). The device allows Gremio to narrate three times the farcical event of the Bible and priest tumbling to the floor; here the repetition renders a comic moment all the more absurd.

Study Questions

1. What does Cambio recite to Bianca?

2. Assess Lucentio's control of Latin.

3. What lesson does Hortensio give to Bianca?

4. Why does Hortensio lose interest so suddenly in Bianca?

5. Why is Kate upset on her wedding day?

6. Why does Petruchio arrive underdressed for his own marriage?

7. What happens during the ceremony?

8. Why does Petruchio insist that he must leave immediately?

9. To which poet does Shakespeare allude in Petruchio's speech about a wife's duty to her husband?

10. How do the guests react to the newlyweds' early departure?

Answers

1. He recites a few lines from Ovid's epistolary poem the *Heroides.*

2. We cannot judge his skill with Latin. Lucentio and Bianca don't try to translate the lines they read.

3. As the musician Lito, Hortensio devises a message, much like that of Lucentio, based upon the arpeggios of the scales. But Bianca notices a minor error in its beginning and rejects it.

4. Bianca has just rejected him, and she begins to show favoritism to the younger schoolmaster.

5. Petruchio fails to show up at the appointed time.

6. He is presumably trying to humiliate Kate, whom he perceives to be spoiled.

7. We learn from Gremio that Petruchio has struck the priest for fumbling the Bible, and that he has given Kate a roaring kiss.

8. He never provides a full explanation.

9. By juxtaposing the words *field* and *barn*, Shakespeare alludes to Richard Barnfield, whose *Affectionate Shephard* had just been published the year of *Shrew's* first known performance. His sonnets probably circulated among the nobility and close friends, who perhaps included Shakespeare.

10. After entreating Petruchio to stay for the banquet, they remain to enjoy the meal.

Suggested Essay Topics

1. Compare Bianca's behavior in Act Three, Scene I with Kate's behavior in Acts I and II. How are the two sisters different in demeanor and attitude in this act?

2. Contrast Petruchio's method of taming his bride as shown in Act III, Scene 2 with his courtship of Kate in Act II. Is the change in tactics warranted? Is it effective?

3. Evaluate Petruchio's speech about a husband's rights over his spouse. How persuasive would his argument be to a modern audience?

SECTION SIX

Act IV

Act IV, Scenes 1 and 2

New characters:

Curtis: *servant of Petruchio who speaks with Grumio*

Nathaniel, Philip, Nicholas, Peter: *servants of Petruchio*

Pedant: *a traveler whom Tranio tricks into playing the role of Vincentio*

Summary

In Act IV, Scene i, Grumio arrives at Petruchio's country home ahead of his master and new mistress to prepare for their reception and, above all, to start a fire to warm the travellers after their chilling journey. He meets Curtis, a fellow servant, who asks whether Katharina is the shrew she is reported to be. Grumio responds that once she was, but that the cold journey has temporarily tamed her.

After some verbal scuffling with Curtis, Grumio reports that Katharina fell into the mud, that Petruchio started to beat him for this nuisance, and that Kate had to intervene to save him from Petruchio. Curtis acknowledges that Petruchio is more of a shrew than Katharina.

Petruchio arrives and scolds Grumio for not bringing the servants to meet him and Kate in a nearby park. Grumio claims that most of the servants were not equipped to meet them.

During Grumio's explanation, a servant tries to offer water to

Kate in order to help her wash up from the journey, but he spills the water. When Petruchio becomes enraged, Kate vainly intervenes to check his anger.

The servants finally bring out supper, but Petruchio claims that the mutton is burnt. Kate objects that the meal has been prepared properly and that the meat is edible. Still, Petruchio insists that burnt meat is bad for choleric tempers like theirs and must be sent back. Petruchio effectively starves Katharina on her first night in her new home.

When Kate has gone to her room in disappointment, Petruchio soliloquizes, revealing his plan to tame Kate by denying her food and sleep.

In Act IV, Scene ii, the courting continues back at Baptista's home. Tranio attempts to dissuade Hortensio from wooing Bianca any further. He suggests that she has already chosen the schoolmaster Cambio. Hortensio agrees, pointing out Bianca's favoritism while eavesdropping on Lucentio and Bianca, who have all but dropped the pretense of poetry lessons.

When Tranio feigns indignation, Hortensio reveals his true identity. The pair forswear Bianca, and Hortensio states that he will pursue a wealthy widow instead.

Hortensio leaves, and Tranio calls to Bianca and Lucentio, who rejoice that Hortensio is now out of the picture. Tranio jokes that Hortensio has gone to taming school. Bianca questions the existence of such a thing, and Tranio responds that Petruchio is the master of one.

Biondello interrupts their felicitations to report that he has seen an old traveler who might fit the part of Vincentio and consent to Lucentio's marriage before Bianca's father. Tranio convinces Lucentio that he will be able to persuade the pedant, by means of a ruse, to assume the identity of Lucentio's father.

Tranio encounters the pedant alone and delivers his story. He says that if the authorities catch the pedant in Padua, they will execute him. The pedant is from Mantua, and the dukes of Padua and Mantua are quarreling. Tranio suggests that the pedant take on the identity of "his" father, Vincentio. The pedant agrees. Tranio further stipulates that he will have to pretend to consent to Tranio's marriage.

Analysis

Although he appears idiotic, Grumio may in fact demonstrate some savvy in Act IV, Scene i by his report of Petruchio's taming technique. He claims, for instance, that "winter tames man, woman and beast" (20), perhaps implying that Petruchio has kept Kate out in the cold in order to break her spirit before she arrives at her new home.

Grumio may not realize, however, the extent to which Petruchio relies upon maltreating him in order to win Kate's support for her new household servants and thus her new living situation. For example, Grumio does not quite play along with Petruchio's irascible behavior when Petruchio beats him for allowing Kate's horse to fall in the mud, or when the servant spills water and receives a lashing.

Still, Shakespeare uses the figure of Grumio for clever comic effect. Note the classical rhetorical device at this point of the extended *paraleipsis*, also called *occupatio* (besieging an audience with details), wherein Grumio insists that he will not tell what happened on their trip but does so anyway (lines 64-75). This rhetorical device allows an orator to have it both ways, that is, to pester an audience with details it may not want to hear, and to claim to save an audience the displeasure of hearing them. A famous example of o*ccupatio* occurs in Chaucer's *The Knight's Tale*, lines 2919-66, where Chaucer masterfully extends one sentence over forty-seven lines. It is possible that Shakespeare's idiotic Grumio owes something to Chaucer's bumbling narrator.

The psychology Petruchio uses in this scene has the desired effect. If he wants Kate to adjust to her new home and feel that it belongs somehow to her, not just to Petruchio, then his strategy of castigating servants succeeds. Kate is tricked into defending servants whom she might have otherwise chastized herself.

As for nearly torturing Kate, Peter reports that this strategy merely mimics Kate's own behavior toward others; he claims that Petruchio "kills her in her own humor" (168). In his soliloquy, Petruchio states the terms for his treatment of Kate: he will deal with her as if she were an animal. Using behavior modification psychology, Petruchio will try to reshape Kate's attitude toward him.

He compares her to a hawk which should fly off to hunt down animals or come at his call. The comparison seems strange here, but the metaphor carries great weight. The hawking metaphor here foreshadows the play's final scene where Petruchio commands Kate to tear apart, figuratively speaking, the two women who will not obey their husbands. The reader will also recall the Lord in the Induction, who had just returned from hunting and was entertaining himself by molding Christopher Sly.

To remind the audience of the Induction at this point, the playwright has Curtis report that Kate responds to Petruchio's treatment "as one new-risen from a dream" (174), a clear allusion to Christopher Sly.

Act IV, Scene ii is purely "connective," or structural. It ties up loose ends and ensures the successful progress of the Lucentio-Bianca subplot.

Hortensio falls to Tranio's original plan to discourage other suitors from competing with Lucentio for Bianca's hand in marriage. In the process, Tranio exposes a trade secret of chauvinism when he exclaims, "Unconstant womankind" (14), a common misogynist charge, repeated anciently by Virgil in his *Aeneid*. In that instance, Mercury has been sent by Jupiter to persuade Aeneas to leave Dido (whom Lucentio referred to at I, i, 54), and claims, "*varium et mutabile semper/ femina*" (woman is ever capricious, 4.569-70). This patriarchal tactic of vilifying women is revealed through Tranio's situation, for he himself, along with Hortensio and Lucentio, is in disguise and appears consummately variable.

This irony is heightened when Tranio invents a convoluted lie to persuade the pedant to pretend to be someone he is not. Both men are willing to employ dishonest means to achieve their ends, whether to help another person, as in the case of Tranio, or to save one's skin, as in the case of the pedant.

It is not surprising at this point in the play that the schoolmaster Cambio mentions Ovid's *Art to Love* (itself variously known as the *Ars Amatoria* and *Ars Amandi*). While his *Metamorphoses*, with its myths of legendary figures, may be a key subtext behind most of Shakespeare's works, Ovid's *Art of Love* (as it is now called) clearly informs this play. The *Art of Love* retells some of the stories from the *Metamorphoses* (such as that of Cephalus, the hunter, and his wife, Procris), but it also emphasizes the idea of fashioning behavior to achieve the desired result in amatory relations. This is a comic text, however, as the narrator/instructor sometimes gives advice that cannot possibly be followed. While knowledge of this work is not necessary to appreciate *The Taming of the Shrew*, any reader familiar with Ovid's classic will see how Shakespeare playfully ridicules lovers in the same fashion as his ancient literary predecessor. Both authors put lovers in compromising situations to test them. Such tests are ludicrous to the audience, however, since it knows that this is just a play and that acting is the basic object anyway.

Study Questions

1. Why does Grumio arrive ahead of Petruchio and Kate?

2. How was their journey from Padua?

3. What do Kate and Petruchio eat when they arrive?

4. Why does Petruchio reject the mutton?

5. What plan does Petruchio concoct to tame Kate after he rejects their meal?

6. Which Ovidian text does Lucentio name to Bianca?

7. Why does Tranio swear not to court Bianca?

8. What is the taming school to which Tranio refers?

9. Why is origin of the pedant important to Tranio?

10. Why does the pedant offer to play the part of Vincentio while in Padua?

Answers

1. He has been sent ahead to start a fire and to prepare servants to meet Petruchio in a park.

2. Grumio's account suggests it was a miserable, cold trip with Kate falling down with her horse into mud.

3. Although a large meal is served, Petruchio sends the entire meal back to the kitchen, and they eat nothing.

4. He claims that it is burnt.

5. Petruchio plans to deny Katharina sleep and to harrass her until she submits to his will.

6. The *Art to Love*, more commonly translated as the *Art of Love*, is the text.

7. Ostensibly, Tranio forswears Bianca because Hortensio has proven her to be attached to Cambio. But since this was Tranio's original plan, he is presumably happy to stop pretending to court Bianca.

8. Tranio merely jokes about Petruchio demonstrating the way to make a wife obey her husband.

9. The actual origin of the pedant is irrelevant, for Tranio could have used any town in his story to fool the pedant.

10. Tranio invents a story that the pedant will be executed unless he disguises his true identity as a Mantuan.

Suggested Essay Topics

1. Describe the methods Petruchio uses to tame Kate in Act IV, Scene 1.

2. Review Grumio's behavior thus far in the play and evaluate his knowledge of his situation.

3. Enumerate the motives of Hortensio and Tranio in agreeing to forswear Bianca. You will need to consider the action in previous scenes to formulate a response.

Act IV, Scene 3 and 4

Summary

In Act IV, Scene iii, Grumio talks with Katharina after a night of terror. We learn from their conversation that Petruchio has fulfilled his plan not to allow his bride any sleep on her wedding night, supposedly "all in the name of perfect love" (12). The scene begins, however, with Grumio denying Kate's request for food. Grumio either believes Petruchio when he claims that certain foods are too choleric for fierce people like Kate, or Grumio is in on the scheme, as he dismisses any food Kate mentions as being too hot or choleric for her temperament. In either case, Grumio sadistically teases Kate by offering, then rejecting, certain foods.

Petruchio enters along with Hortensio, and tantalizes Kate with a real piece of food. Petruchio uses Kate's silence at this point to give the meat to Hortensio, stating that Kate has not thanked him for his kind offer. Clearly, Kate did not believe he would ever give it to her.

A tailor and haberdasher enter with a gown and cap respectively. When Petruchio rejects the cap, Kate defies him and declares that the cap suits the current fashion. Petruchio maintains his position, and an enraged Kate starts to launch a harangue against Petruchio. He cuts her off, ignores what she has said, and pretends that Katharina has agreed with him.

Petruchio rejects the tailor's gown in a similar manner, but this time he argues with the tailor not Kate. In fact, when Kate charges Petruchio with making a puppet of her, he displaces the blame onto the tailor. Petruchio finally dismisses the tailor, but sends Hortensio to pay him for his trouble. Petruchio justifies his action by telling Kate that they must appear humble before her father.

Petruchio announces his plans for departure, but Kate points out that he has mistaken the time of day in his calculations. Petruchio becomes indignant and refuses to leave until his calculations are accepted and demonstrated.

In Act IV, Scene iv, Tranio and the pedant arrive at Baptista's to perform the act of consent. The pedant worries, however, that Baptista may recognize him from their meeting some twenty years ago.

Baptista greets them and Tranio hastily asks for his "father's" consent to marry Bianca. The pedant feigns a more graceful approach to the business of their union and his consent, but speedily gives his consent anyway.

Baptista urges them to proceed more cautiously, since the dowry arrangements have not yet been made. He asks that they not discuss these matters at his house for fear of eavesdroppers, such as Gremio. Tranio suggests that they transact their negotiations at his lodging where his father is staying.

At this point, Baptista sends Lucentio off to inform Bianca of their dealings and to get her ready to greet her fiancé formally. Tranio, Baptista, and the pedant leave for dinner. Biondello appears while Lucentio is still on stage, and alerts Lucentio to Tranio's presumed plans. Biondello implies that Lucentio must marry Bianca before they hold the binding church ceremony. Lucentio leaves to fetch Bianca.

Analysis

Act IV, Scene iii shows a darker side to Petruchio and Grumio, who at this point seems to be collaborating with his master; Grumio certainly follows Petruchio's lead, in any case. Given Kate's admission that she has never had to ask for anything in her life (7-8), Petruchio's method seems fitted to the task of disciplining a spoiled person.

With the cap incident, Petruchio specifies how Kate will have to act in order to get what she wants—she will have to be *gentle* (71). Here Petruchio puns on the double sense of "gentle," which can mean either mild or noble. He suggests, then, that Kate's lack of mildness undermines the honor of her *bourgeois* origins. For an Elizabethan audience attuned to self-conscious theatrical signals, Petruchio's gesture signals that many of the players on stage are dressing above their station when they perform.

This metatheatrical signal is repeated when Grumio mistakes Petruchio's meaning in the statement, "the gown is not for me" (151). Grumio absurdly thinks that Petruchio had thought that the gown was for him to wear. This idea recalls the situation involving Bartholomew in the Induction and reminds an Elizabethan audience that every "woman" on the stage is a crossdressed boy.

Bringing attention to the common Shakespearean theme of the falsity of mere appearances, Petruchio decides that the couple will return to Padua in humble clothing. Petruchio's attitude toward the world of appearances, however, is not necessarily negative. As he tried to create a new reality with his novel descriptions by flattering Kate in the wooing scene, so Petruchio insists here that the time will be whatever he declares it to be. Furthermore, the gown which he has meticulously ordered no longer suits his pleasure. He will not allow Kate to cross his will no matter how mad it may seem. This attitude leads Kate to reflect accurately that Petruchio "mean[s] to make a puppet" of her (103). Indeed, just as in the wooing scene, Petruchio sometimes ignores anything negative coming from Kate and seems to hear only what he wishes her to say. He appears on his way to fashioning a *model* wife, in both senses of the word—namely, a wife who will prove an *example* to others, and a wife who is more *puppet* than a person.

Act IV, Scene iv is a short scene which develops the subplot of the dual set of marriage preparations. Not only must Tranio arrange to marry Bianca publicly, but Lucentio needs to wed Bianca in secret before the binding public ceremony. Otherwise, the audience is left to assume, the servant will be lawfully married to Bianca, leaving the aspiring Lucentio out in the cold.

The terms Biondello uses to describe the elopement are not flattering to Bianca, or to women. He refers to Bianca metaphorically as a book to which his master must gain the rights before it goes into publication; otherwise, any man whatsoever will still be able to claim her as his own. By marrying Bianca in secret, any subsequent marriage would only be a "counterfeit" and, therefore, worthless. This metaphor, which compares women to books (or, more accurately, manuscripts), has a long and sordid history. No matter what its ugly permutations, the metaphor equates men with an active principle and women with a receptive, inactive one. To expand this version of the metaphor, the woman is the parchment upon which the active male writes his story.

In order to ensure that a story is not changed or copied by a rival, the writer must seek a copyright. Books, of course, had only recently become available in England. Caxton had brought his printing press to England and printed the first book in English around 1474. Problems of publication and authenticity were still cause for considerable anxiety, as the history of this text attests (see the Theatrical Background section of the Introduction). Identifying authorship of manuscripts before books became commonplace was even more difficult as many works were kept anonymous during the Middle Ages. It was customary for several writers to inscribe annotations on a single page of parchment (or vellum) while what we think of as the text occupied less than half of the page's space, and often became obscured.

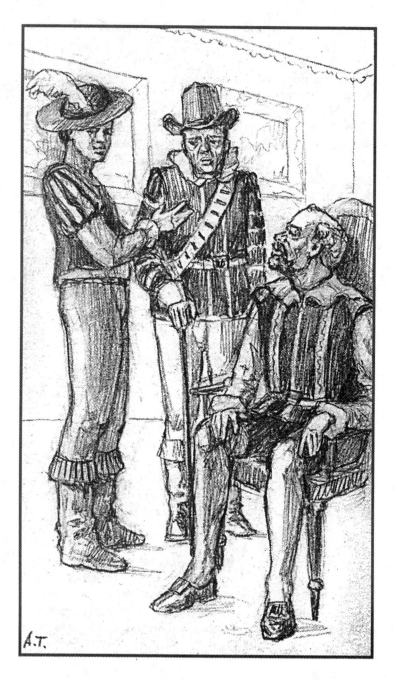

Biondello changes the metaphor slightly by referring to Bianca as Lucentio's "appendix", that is, the tail end of the book. The comparison recalls two moments in the play where Petruchio has been describing the relation he wants to have with Kate. First, Petruchio had joked lewdly of having his tongue in Kate's *tail*, where she had imagined the sting (of her *tale*) to be hidden (II,i,210-18). Later, Petruchio had declared that his wife should be his "ass," his "anything" (IV,i,231). The appendix metaphor, despite its association with a code necessary to interpret the book itself, does not, therefore, show the wife in a favorable light. The careful reader of Elizabethan English will note here that "appendix" sounds suspiciously like "apprentice," and that this verbal variation recalls the fact that boy actors were apprenticed to theatrical companies whereas veterans, such as Richard Burbage, received wages.

Baptista has been easily duped by Tranio and Lucentio. His comment that Bianca and Tranio love each other well, "Or both dissemble deeply their affections" (42), shows ironically how far he has been deceived. In another moment of poignant irony, Biondello characterizes the disguised pedant and Tranio as the "deceiving father of a deceitful son" (82-83). He makes this remark to Lucentio at his expense, for Lucentio is truly the son who is deceiving not only his real father, but also his father-in-law-to-be who, at least according to Lucentio's plan, will never know that he has married Bianca to the schoolmaster and not to Tranio.

Study Questions

1. What does Grumio give to Kate for breakfast?

2. How long has Kate slept on her wedding night?

3. What reason does Petruchio give for rejecting the cap?

4. Does Petruchio accept the gown?

5. When was the last time Kate has eaten?

6. Where did the pedant encounter Baptista twenty years ago?

7. To whom does Baptista think he is giving away his daughter, Bianca?

8. Why does Baptista not make immediate arrangements for Bianca's dowry once he has met the pedant disguised as Vincentio?

9. How will Lucentio be able to marry Bianca before the public ceremony with Tranio as groom to Bianca?

10. To what two things does Biondello compare Bianca when speaking with Lucentio about her?

Answers

1. He gives her not a morsel.

2. She slept not a wink.

3. First he says it is lewd, filthy, and too small; but then he claims that Kate is not gentle enough to wear it.

4. Not according to this text. Petruchio does pay the tailor, but only in the movie version (with Elizabeth Taylor) does he finally accept the dress after he has sent away the tailor.

5. Presumably on the morning of her wedding, at least 24 hours before Grumio taunts her, though probably much more.

6. The pedant encountered Baptista in Genoa.

7. Baptista thinks he will give Bianca to Tranio, who has assumed the name, clothing and character of Lucentio.

8. Baptista wants to make arrangements in private, not on the street, and fears his servants or Gremio might eavesdrop on their negotiations at his house.

9. Lucentio must take Bianca at night to the old priest at Saint Luke's Church where they will be married in secret.

10. First he compares her to a book, then more specifically to the appendix of a book.

Suggested Essay Topics

1. Baptista readily discusses dowry arrangements in Act II, Scene 1. Why, then, does he claim here that he is afraid of too many "ears" in his house? Is Shakespeare merely using

this excuse as a way to get Baptista to encounter the real Vincentio by transporting him to Tranio's lodgings? What makes these two scenes different?

2. Examine the metaphor of the book as applied to a woman, or more specifically to a bride, in Scene 4. What does this metaphor entail? What kind of autonomy does it grant to a woman? Who, for instance, does this comparison assume is writing the book?

Act IV, Scene 5

New Character:

Vincentio—*Lucentio's father, who arrives unexpectedly and foils his son's plans to elope*

Summary

Petruchio, Katharina, Hortensio, and some servants have set out for Padua to attend the wedding of Bianca and Tranio/Lucentio. On the way, Petruchio stops to test Kate's willingness to accept his version of reality. Petruchio comments that the moon shines brightly, but Kate corrects him, saying it is the sun that shines. Petruchio commands that the moon, or some star, shall shine if he says it does before they continue their journey. Hortensio intervenes to warn Kate to let Petruchio have his way. Kate accedes, declaring that the time of day shall be whatever her husband deems but says so only to may move on.

Unsure that he has won the game, Petruchio tests her again, claiming first that the moon, then the sun, shines. Kate agrees in each instance and grants that the day shall be whatever her husband commands. Satisfied, Petruchio allows them to continue their journey.

The group immediately encounters the real Vincentio, an aged man. Petruchio uses this occasion to try Katharina's patience once again. He hails Vincentio as a "gentle mistress," and suggests that Kate do the same. In a speech memorable for its gifted exaggeration, Kate greets the elderly Vincentio as "Young budding virgen,

fair and fresh and sweet." Changing his tack, Petruchio contradicts Kate and signals her to apologize to Vincentio. Kate performs this minor task with the same alacrity and virtuosity of her previous speech to Vincentio.

The test having been settled to his satisfaction, Petruchio asks Vincentio where he is headed. Vincentio informs them that he is bound for Padua to visit his son Lucentio. Thinking of Tranio, Petruchio assures Vincentio that his son is well and about to be married to Bianca, Kate's sister. The anticipated marriage will make Vincentio a kinsman, though not a blood relation, and Petruchio embraces him as such.

When Vincentio becomes outraged that his son has contracted to marry without his consent, Petruchio reassures him that the supposed Lucentio has made a noble match. Vincentio is still incredulous on account of Petruchio's game with Kate which came at his own expense; Hortensio intervenes to affirm Petruchio's story.

After everyone else has left the stage, Hortensio soliloquizes that he has learned how to tame his widow by Petruchio's guiding example.

Analysis

This is the first scene that presents Kate as appearing to accept Petruchio's view of reality, even if that means defying reality as she knows it. But this capitulation may not be entirely binding, for it seems to mainly allow Petruchio to believe what he wants. We have no way of knowing, in other words, what Kate is actually thinking or what she believes to be true. For example, when Petruchio rants that "It shall be moon, or star, or what [he] list" (7), this statement does not really entail much from Kate. She simply agrees with him, almost certainly without meaning it.

The audience may well ask what good this kind of performance serves. Is this really what men want from their wives, mere mimicry and mindless obedience? Or is there another reason behind Petruchio's gestures? The play's final scene will point to the importance of Kate's public performance of her obedience to Petruchio. In this scene, Shakespeare spends no little effort putting beautiful, if overly ornate, speeches in Kate's mouth, which she performs brilliantly before Vincentio. Is Petruchio bringing out the best in Kate precisely at the point where she gives in to his whims? Or has he forced her to deliver her best as a sort of survival technique?

In any event, the ambiguity presented by Kate's gestures of capitulation, here as well as later in the play, has lead to much debate over what kind of slave Kate has become—whether she fully accepts her mental and physical domination, or whether she is merely playing along to suit her own purposes. The problem for both points of view, obviously, is that the playwright leaves to the audience's imagination to determine what Kate's interests really are. We know what Petruchio wants. What does Kate want?

At this point in the analysis of the play, it must be noted that Shakespeare's audience included a very large number of women. In Spain, on the other hand, women were either discouraged from attending the theater, or were kept separate from men in the audience. (Spain also banned women from acting between 1596 and 1600, and boy actors played the parts of women.) In other words, we should not assume that Shakespeare wrote exclusively for the male imagination. Whether a male playwright could understand the female imagination is not so much at issue, therefore, as is the question of how well he was able to depict or appeal to the concerns of women.

No matter how an audience reckons Kate's attitude, she demonstrates her awareness of Petruchio's game both in the way she develops flowery speech for Vincentio, and in the way she figures Petruchio metaphorically—"And the moon changes even as your mind" (20). In Renaissance symbolism, the moon represents woman, who borrows her strength from man just as the moon borrows its light from the sun. By comparing Petruchio to the moon, Kate equates Petruchio with a woman, and reveals her understanding of his tactics. By playing the part of the fickle woman, Petruchio is trying to beat women at their own game. Such a victory would make him the real master of his house, not simply master in name alone. It will be further noted that Elizabethans were quite anxious about domineering wives and weak husbands, as the relevant laws and ritual punishments reflect.

Hortensio reminds us of this kind of anxiety with his comment, "'A will make the man mad, to make a woman of him."(35) Preying upon this fear, Kate embellishes her greeting to Vincentio by referring to a potential male bedfellow for him. This idea dredges up all the tension in the audience occasioned by the act of crossdressing in the Induction. When countermanded, however, Kate alludes to the metaphor of the sun and moon again. This time, she assigns Petruchio to a man's traditional place in the system: "Pardon, old father, my mistaking eyes,/That have been so bedazzled by the sun..."(44-45). Her comment is meant to be taken both literally and figuratively, and this demonstrates Kate's own sophistication with language, second best only to Petruchio. The remark is construed literally to mean that Kate was momentarily blinded by the bright light of the day, so she saw an old man as a green one, or as a young girl. The switch in sex from old to young is plausible to a Renaissance mind, since notions of maleness and femaleness tended to be grouped with ideas of age: for example, a person is thought of as feminine until he reaches maturity and becomes a masculine man. Figuratively construed, Kate refers to herself as necessarily blinded by the demands of her husband, who is compared to the sun. Thus, Kate alerts the audience to the fact that she only says what Petruchio tells her to; she does not take him seriously at this point.

Hortensio makes a comparison of his own, which equates Kate with a *field* to be won or lost during a war. The metaphor assumes yet another, older one where the woman represents the fields that lie fallow until a man comes along to till them. Petruchio, not so happy with Hortensio's completely banal comparison, suggests one from the game of bowling. A game metaphor is not so unusual if we recall his references to hawking, another pursuit for those with leisure. In his metaphor, it is assumed that Kate should not roll against the bias. Petruchio thus thinks of himself as the portion of a bowling ball which weights it, thereby influencing its path. It would be interesting to speculate here how Petruchio conceptualizes Kate, whether as an active bowler, or as a passive bowling pin, that is, as an obstacle. An answer would shed light on how much independence she possesses while she continues to take orders from her demanding husband.

Study Questions

1. What time of day is it when Petruchio declares that the moon shines bright?

2. Whom do Kate and Petruchio encounter on their journey?

3. How does Kate give in to Petruchio?

4. Why is Vincentio headed to Padua?

5. To what does Petruchio refer when he mentions being crossed?

6. How does Petruchio greet Vincentio?

7. How does Kate earn Petruchio's favor when meeting Vincentio?

8. How does Vincentio respond to their games with him?

9. Why is Hortensio with Kate and Petruchio?

10. What does Hortensio plan to do when he returns to Padua?

Answers

1. It is daytime.

2. They meet Lucentio's real father, Vincentio.

3. Kate reports what Petruchio says to be true, although it is notably false. She later performs according to his will in front of Vincentio.

4. Vincentio wishes to visit with his son, whom he has not seen in a long while.

5. He alludes to Kate's practice of contradicting him when he lies or is otherwise testing her patience.

6. He greets Vincentio in an exaggeratedly cordial way and also refers to Vincentio as a woman.

7. Kate greets Vincentio as a woman, following Petruchio's lead. She then apologizes for her behavior when Petruchio contradicts her for mistaking Vincentio as a woman.

8. Vincentio is notably confused. He refuses to believe Petruchio

when he later claims that Vincentio is his kinsman by
Lucentio's marriage to Bianca.

9. Hortensio admits at the end of this scene that he has been
    watching Petruchio's skill at taming women.

10. He is eager to test his taming tricks on a wealthy widow after
    she agrees to marry him.

Suggested Essay Topics

1. Examine Kate's autonomy after her capitulation to
    Petruchio's whims. How much freedom does she sacrifice
    by placating Petruchio's perverse sense of humor?

2. Consider the many comparisons used in this scene. In what
    sort of light do they cast the people they describe? For
    example, how does Hortensio's metaphor of the field depict
    Kate?

3. Reflect upon the tension involving gender (masculine ver-
    sus feminine roles) in this scene. What are the pivotal mo-
    ments in this play when gender becomes an issue for us?
    Develop a few questions that would occur to a modern au-
    dience for each situation.

Act V

Act V, Scene 1 and 2

Summary

In Act V, Scene i, Gremio lurks in front of Lucentio's house, but apparently does not see Lucentio, Bianca, or Biondello as they steal away to the church for the secret marriage ceremony. While Tranio and the pedant are still inside, Petruchio, Kate, and Vincentio reach Lucentio's home and knock. Gremio comes out from hiding to inform them that they had best knock more loudly since those within are busy.

The pedant appears at the window above the front door, and greets Vincentio in a hostile manner. After Petruchio announces that Lucentio's father, Vincentio, has just arrived from Pisa and wants to see his son, the pedant calls him a liar and claims that he himself is Lucentio's father. The pedant then demands that Vincentio be restrained and brought before the law.

Biondello approaches the house and realizes that his master's plot will be ruined if the pedant is exposed as an imposter. Vincentio recognizes Biondello and orders him to come forward, but Biondello pretends that he has never met Vincentio before. When Biondello points to the pedant in the window as his master, Vincentio starts to beat him and he runs off stage. Petruchio moves himself and Kate out of the action to watch what will happen.

Tranio, still dressed up as his master, finally comes out of the house, to the consternation of Vincentio. He laments that Lucentio has wasted his money on his servant to furnish him with such rich

apparel. Tranio announces his identity as a gentleman, and Vincentio reproaches him, claiming that his father was a sailmaker. Baptista tries to intervene and calm the rising confusion by asking Vincentio to identify Tranio. Vincentio declares it to be Tranio, and the pedant defends Tranio as Lucentio. This convinces Vincentio that Tranio has murdered his son and assumed his identity. Tranio is forced, therefore, to call for an officer to arrest Vincentio, because Tranio has been accused of murder.

The officer arrives, but Gremio steps in to defend Vincentio. However, since Gremio will not swear that Tranio is not Lucentio, Baptista asks that Vincentio be carried away to jail. At this point, Lucentio, Bianca, and Biondello appear to find Vincentio constrained by the constable. Biondello warns Lucentio not to give away their scheme. Then Tranio, Biondello, and the pedant run quickly off stage.

Lucentio kneels before his father to ask for pardon. Bianca does likewise before her own father. Lucentio reveals his identity to Baptista, then explains to his father how he planned to use Tranio to woo Bianca. Lucentio begs his father's forgiveness for his deception and he assumes responsibility for the acts of Tranio and Biondello. Vincentio forgives him, but goes into the house to be avenged upon the two servants who would have him taken to jail.

Baptista, followed by Lucentio and Bianca, exits. Gremio is left behind to marvel that he has come up empty-handed. Once he goes in to the banquet, Kate and Petruchio are left on stage. Petruchio asks Kate for a kiss, but she admonishes him that such a thing would not be proper in public. Once Petruchio tells Grumio to pack up to return home, Kate cuts off their preparations and gives Petruchio a kiss in the street. Petruchio rejoices and they exit the stage.

In Act V, Scene ii, Lucentio gives a short speech to begin the wedding banquet at which Bianca, Baptista, Petruchio, Kate, Gremio, Hortensio, and his newly-wedded widow are all present. Petruchio grumbles that they must always sit down, and a conversation ensues, which is difficult to follow because of the frequent use of innuendo. The men banter somewhat separately from the women, but both groups engage in the same form of witty linguistic one-upmanship. One notable instance is a comment from the

widow, who implies that Petruchio is a hypocrite for claiming that Hortensio is afraid of her. Petruchio lets her remark go by without chastising her, but Kate calls the widow on her charge by asking what she means by it. The widow tries to dodge Kate's question, but when pressed again, the widow chooses to be frank.

With the widow's claim of Katharina's shrewishness now obvious to everyone, Petruchio instructs Kate to attack the widow verbally. Hortensio also exhorts his bride to do likewise. Petruchio and Hortensio then bet on their wives' success in the contest.

Attention shifts suddenly to Baptista, who asks Gremio whether he is enjoying the conversation so far. His reply allows Bianca an opportunity to insinuate that he is a cuckhold. Seeing that Bianca has entered the fray, Petruchio announces to her that she too is fair game for their verbal sparring. Bianca puts his idea to rest by exiting. Kate and the widow follow.

Without missing a beat, Petruchio puns on the fact that the women have walked away from the men in order to poke at Tranio and Gremio, the men who courted and missed their targets. Tranio compares himself to a greyhound who hunts for his master, and Petruchio first compliments, then sneers at his simile. Tranio, re-employing his metaphor, quips that Petruchio is thought to be held at bay by his new wife. The men chuckle at this, but Petruchio appears poised to humiliate them by questioning the obedience of their wives. Petruchio wagers that his wife is the most loyal; to prove it, he suggests that they call their wives to them in succession. Lucentio bets twenty crowns. Petruchio says that he would bet as much on an animal of his, but would stake twenty times more on his wife. Chagrined, Lucentio ups his bet to one hundred crowns. The men agree. Baptista offers to go in for half of Lucentio's expense, but is refused.

Lucentio calls to Bianca first and is rejected. Hortensio makes the attempt, yet fares no better. Petruchio sends Biondello specifically to *command* Kate to return to him, and she obeys. The men are stunned except, of course, for Petruchio, who then orders Kate to bring out the widow and Bianca. At this point, Baptista exclaims that he now has a new daughter and offers Petruchio a second dowry of 20,000 crowns.

Petruchio orders Kate to doff her cap and crush it underfoot. She obeys, and the women complain of her treatment by Petruchio. Both Lucentio and Hortensio upbraid their wives for disobeying them and are met with haughty replies.

Petruchio then tells Kate to chastise each wife, starting with the widow, for treating their masters so rudely. In a t*our de force* of verbal showmanship, Kate explains at length why women must serve their husbands with a smile. She then drops to the ground and offers to take up her husband's boot in her hands. Petruchio, presumably lifting Kate up from her kneeling posture, rejoices and kisses Kate in front of the others. The men marvel at Kate's new behavior. Once Petruchio and Kate exit, the new husbands admire Petruchio's taming of Kate once again.

Analysis

In Act V, Scene i, the expected complication in the subplot reaches its climax with the arrival of the real father. Lucentio's plan to marry Bianca, by having Tranio go through the public ceremony in his place, is exposed. This plot was not Shakespeare's own invention, as the allusion to Gascoigne's English version of Ariosto's *I Suppositi* (Supposes) attests. Lucentio says that "counterfeit supposes" (meaning disguises, 110) have tricked the others into believing that Tranio was Lucentio. Lucentio seems to shift the blame away from himself, however, when he claims that "Love wrought these miracles" (116).

Some of the tension caused by dressing beyond one's station is here at play as well. Note Vincentio's reaction to Tranio's clothing when he encounters him (60-65).

Once the stage has been cleared and only Petruchio, Kate, and Grumio remain, Petruchio tests Kate for the last time by asking her for a kiss in public. She protests but ultimately gives in. Petruchio celebrates his victory over her. He looks forward to the banquet where he will show off his hard work before the other men, who, he knows, will scrutinize Kate's behavior toward her new husband.

This scene also employs a dramatic "cascade effect," as characters leave the stage in a staggered order. This device suggests the complex nature of the plots that overlap here. Of course, the threater audience would also see Christopher Sly, who is presumably asleep up in his loft overlooking the main stage.

As one might expect, Act V, Scene ii serves as the focus of attention for those who are interested in gender relations in the Elizabethan period as represented in this play. Two points seem pressing here: why must Kate kneel and offer her hands for Petruchio's boots; and why should Kate be made to argue for her own subservience to her husband?

Again, critical opinion splits over the question of Kate's sincerity. Some people view Kate as thoroughly brainwashed and dominated by Petruchio. Others choose to believe that Kate is merely performing the role assigned to her, one she enacted before Vincentio. According to this view, she retains her own self respect and true identy since she does not believe in male supremacy.

At least two other interpretations of Kate's position are possible. First, Kate may suggest that no real autonomy (or individual freedom) is possible anyway since every person alive is always already *subject* to a prince. According to this way of thinking, freedom becomes a relative term. No absolute independence, or autonomy, exists—even the prince is accountable to the people in some fashion. Another reading of this scene might claim that Kate is aware of her situation and has assessed that all women are outmatched by men because men are generally more shrewish than women. This reading is supported by Kate's earlier comparisons of Petruchio with the moon, a lunatic, and so on.

Petruchio, for his part, anticipates that Kate may very well be playing her assigned role, for he forces her to crush her cap underfoot as a "*sign* of her obedience"(119). Ironically, however, he calls Kate's efforts to bring the wives out from the parlor her "womanly persuasion"(122). This name begs the question of whose skill is being employed to command women.

A further irony stems from Kate's argument that women's bodies are unfit for labor or command:

Why are our bodies soft and weak and smooth,
Unapt to toil and trouble in the world,
But that our soft conditions and our hearts
Should well agree with our external parts? (167-170)

An Elizabethan audience will recognize that while, on one level, Kate assumes that the body mirrors the condition of the mind, her subject matter, on another level, is ironic because Kate is really a boy dressed as a woman. Kate's argument betrays her at this moment because her words about women's bodies point ludricrously to a male's body instead. It is not difficult to imagine the boy who plays Kate signalling this fact to the audience's attention with a wry smile or some simple disclosing gesture.

The matter of cross-dressing aside, whatever our view of Kate's sincerity, the audience will notice that she has uttered the longest speech in the play and earns the most acclaim for it. Her gift for witty repartee has apparently been transformed into the cautious gracefulness of a person who knows when to stay quiet and when to vent her spleen in a controlled way. Once she is judged to be tamed—something the audience can never quite know—Kate really appears to have mastered herself and to have harnessed the ability to create a compelling argument. This achievement puts into relief the lowly kind of repartee those around Kate enjoy rather frivolously. With this in mind, Kate appears serious and conscientious while the rest, including Petruchio, seem cheap and, at times, contemptible.

In this final scene, Bianca's behavior seems to change, but the audience will find that she has played her part exquisitely all along. She has been more coy than shrewish, though this scene certainly questions the difference in motivation for each form of behavior. Clearly, Shakespeare paints Bianca in this scene as a kind of tramp. Note, for instance, how quick she is to call Gremio a cuckhold then tell the men that they are "welcome all" (48) when they mean to hunt her with verbal assault. This comment portrays her as teasing the men whom she enjoys luring.

The matter of the wager, as was remarked earlier, recalls the story of Lucretia, whose husband eagerly bets on her chastity and dutifulness. In that apocryphal story, told first by Livy in his history of early Rome, all of the wives except for Lucretia have been found lacking in duty to their husbands. One of those unfortunate husbands, Sextus Tarquinius, comes back later to make love to Lucretia, who rejects him. He rapes her, and Lucretia commits suicide because she cannot live knowing that her body has been violated. Enraged by the atrocity, a man named Brutus comes forward to demand that Romans put down the Tarquin family of kings, who have enslaved their people. Brutus' bravery here stuns everyone because he had affected insanity up to that time. His act of

bravery and dissimulation earned Brutus the reputation of being a very shrewd man, a feature not uncharacteristic of Petruchio, who has had to play the part of a "mad-brain rudesby" (III,ii,10) and one "half lunatic" (II,i,284) in order to convince Kate to obey him.

Study Questions

1. Why is Gremio present in this scene?
2. Where is Tranio's father from?
3. Why does Vincentio think that Lucentio has wasted his fortune while in Padua?
4. Why does Vincentio accuse Tranio of murdering Lucentio?
5. Why is Gremio eager to defend Vincentio?
6. Why does Tranio call for a constable?
7. Who finally gives away Lucentio's scheme to marry Bianca privately?
8. How much time has passed since Petruchio and Kate were married?
9. How much money has Baptista lost on account of Petruchio's bet with the husbands?
10. According to Kate, why should women obey their husbands?

Answers

1. He is apparently eavesdropping on Cambio, his rival.
2. Being a sailmaker in Bergamo, Tranio's father is presumably from there.
3. Since Tranio is dressed up beyond the station of a servant, Vincentio thinks that Lucentio has spent money on him.
4. Once Tranio claims that he himself is Lucentio, the only logical possibility that occurs to Vincentio is that Tranio has killed his master.
5. Tranio (as Lucentio) is Gremio's rival, and Gremio probably wants to discredit him as much as possible in order to win Baptista's approval to marry Bianca.

6. Although the pedant has already done so, Tranio waits until there is no other option but to have Vincentio forciably removed so that the wedding arrangements with Baptista will go forward.

7. Lucentio gives it away.

8. Exactly one week has passed since they were married.

9. Though Lucentio turned down Baptista's offer to meet half of his bet in case Bianca should not obey him, Baptista also offers a second dowry for Kate, which amounts to 20,000 crowns; it is unclear whether Petruchio accepts the money, however.

10. To summarize, women are obligated to serve their husbands in the same way every subject owes allegiance to the prince; service merely shows simple gratitude for a husband's hard work; women's bodies are not suited to labor, and, therefore, women must obey the men, who labor on their behalf; women are no physical match for men.

Suggested Essay Topics

1. Enumerate all the stories that Vincentio is forced to accept as truth. Be sure to include Act IV, Scene 5 in your account.

2. How is Kate treated in Act V, Scene 2? How does Kate behave considering the ways in which people treat her?

3. Outline Kate's argument for male supremacy. Does her argument make sense? Is Kate speaking sincerely here, or is she merely saying what Petruchio wants to hear?

Sample Analytical Paper Topics

The following theses and outlines are provided to help you construct successful paper topics and to organize essays which reflect the complexity of the text. These outlines can also aid your efforts to review the play's critical themes and issues.

Topic #1

Many characters in *The Taming of the Shrew* take on different identities, while the behavior of two characters changes drastically by the end of the play. Describe three to four ways in which *The Taming of the Shrew* develops the idea that appearances should not be confused with reality.

Outline

I.   Thesis Statement: *In* The Taming of the Shrew, *Shakespeare develops the theme of appearances versus reality by means of the Induction, disguises, and changes in attitude of the major characters.*

II. Appearance versus reality in the Induction

    A.   The Lord dresses Sly as a nobleman.

    B.   The Lord's page, Bartholomew, is presented as Sly's wife.

    C.   Crossdressing was used in original performances of *Shrew*.

        1.   Petruchio points to Kate as a boy twice.

      2. Biondello alludes to Bianca as a boy with his pun on "appendix."

      3. Kate signals that she is really a boy in her long speech.

III. Disguises suggest that appearances cannot be relied upon.

    A. Lucentio and Hortensio assume identities below their station.

    B. Tranio and the Pedant pretend to be wealthy men.

    C. Shakespeare uses the theme of "counterfeit supposes," taken from another English playwright, as his own device.

IV. Remarkable shifts in behavior alert the audience to the possibility of masquerade and deception.

    A. Petruchio flatters and then harrasses Kate, as if in a game.

    B. Kate alters her behavior to please Petruchio, but the audience may not be convinced of her sincerity.

    C. Petruchio seems interested only in appearances.

      1. He explains to the men that he and Kate will fight openly while treating each other cordially in private.

      2. He appears concerned more with his image before the other men than with developing a sincere relationship with Kate.

    D. Grumio imitates Petruchio in an absurd way. This also suggests that Petruchio may be doing the same, but convincingly so.

    E. Bianca behaves coyly, then becomes a shrewish wife at the play's end.

V. Conclusion: Through the behavior and disguises of the characters, as well as the crossdressing on the Elizabethan stage, *The Taming of the Shrew* emphasizes that appearances are easily mistaken for reality, both in life and in the theater.

Topic #2

In *The Taming of the Shrew*, Petruchio employs various strategies to trick or to coerce his wife into obedience. Describe the methods Petruchio uses to tame his "shrew," and evaluate his effectiveness.

Outline

I. Thesis Statement: *Though Petruchio employs several means of taming Kate, it is ultimately unclear how much success he enjoys.*

II. Petruchio flatters Kate and uses reverse psychology to trick her into not only believing that he loves her, but also into being obedient to him.

    A.   Flattery in the wooing scene.

    B.   Petruchio defends Kate's image before the other men.

    C.   Before the wedding banquet, Petruchio defends Kate against the other men, who, he pretends, are trying to steal his bride from him.

III. Petruchio physically forces Kate to accept him and to be obedient.

    A.   He starves her on her wedding night.

    B.   He humiliates and thereby humbles Kate.

        1.   Petruchio comes to his own wedding dressed in tatters.

        2.   He denies Kate a fashionable dress and cap.

        3.   Petruchio orders Kate to submit to him before the other husbands.

    C.   Petruchio will not let Kate have her way unless it accords with his plans.

        1.   He will not leave his country home until Kate agrees with his pronouncements about the time of day.

        2.   Petruchio vows to take Kate home on the day of Bianca's wedding banquet unless Kate gives him a kiss in public.

IV. Petruchio plays psychological games with Kate in order to test her obedience.

    A. He ignores whatever she says if it does not agree with his desires.

        1. The wooing scene, alone and before the men

        2. The dress and cap

    B. He tests her obedience.

        1. The time of day

        2. Vincentio as a maiden

        3. The public kiss before the banquet

V. Petruchio only seems successful; many things suggest that he has, in fact, failed to tame Kate completely.

    A. If Petruchio only wanted outward displays of obedience and agreement, then he has successfully tamed Kate. Kate finally does what he says and agrees with him on several things that are notably false.

        1. She agrees that the moon shines during the day.

        2. She kisses him in public twice.

        3. She pretends that Vincentio is a maiden.

        4. At the play's end, she comes to Petruchio and brings out the other wives from the parlor.

        5. She recites a hyperbolic speech about a wife's obedience to her husband.

    B. Gestures do not indicate mental states; therefore, one can never know whether Kate accepts Petruchio whole-heartedly.

    C. Kate's speech at the play's end seems over-performed. She is probably play acting for Petruchio here as she did before Vincentio.

    D. Kate is really a boy; taming him is beside the point.

VI. Conclusion: By means of physical coercion, flattery, and trickery, Petruchio manages to force Kate into outward submission. But Kate's true feelings are still unclear to the audience. Thus, Petruchio's victory over Kate remains questionable.

Topic #3

The Taming of the Shrew seems to make a case for male supremacy. But at times this bid for the naturalness of male dominance is overplayed hyperbolic, and treated comically of Shakespeare. Consider the instances of chauvinism in the play and reflect upon the ways in which this play portrays maleness and supremacy.

Outline

I. Thesis Statement: *While* The Taming of the Shrew *includes many scenes of barbaric injustice toward women, the play's overall attitude toward male dominance is both ironic and comic.*

II. Instances of male dominance in this play are exaggerated and should not be taken seriously. These instances suggest that chauvinism is pure performance, not instinctive.

   A. Petruchio's humiliation of Kate is unrealistic.

      1. Starving Kate and depriving her of sleep goes too far.

      2. Petruchio's humiliation of Kate on her wedding day, coupled with his insistence that Vincentio is a maiden and that the moon shines during the day, all challenge the audience's ability to believe in Petruchio's own sincerity.

   B. The hyperbolic intensity of Kate's speech about a wife's subservience to her husband undermines her credibility.

   C. Just as the many disguises in this play point to the possibility of appearances being false, acts of chauvinism begin to look like acts of deception.

   D. The Induction uses the subplot of the Lord deceiving Christopher Sly in order to alert the audience to the art of deception practiced by those in powerful positions.

III. Irony sabotages the audience's view of male supremacy.

   A. The Petrarchism of Petruchio's wooing speeches points up the extent to which he relies upon others for his approach and is indeed acting a part. Masculinity here seems more performed than natural. The fact that Petruchio calls Hortensio and Lucentio "novices" points up the skill (or artifice) he employs.

B.   Grumio's imitation of Petruchio reflects badly upon Petruchio insofar as it will occur to the audience that Petruchio himself had been acting.

C.   The crossdressing in original performances, and in some revivals, completely undermines the notion that sexual attraction is naturally inclined. This uncertainty, in turn, allows the audience to question the naturalness of male dominance.

1.   Sly falls for Bartholomew, dressed as a woman.

2.   Petruchio signals his knowledge that Kate is really a boy.

3.   The fact that only boys can portray women on stage may suggest that men are more innately female than women. If true, the claim that men are superior to women becomes entangled in the question of what maleness truly is.

IV.   Conclusion: *The Taming of the Shrew's* highly ironic view of male supremacy suggests that male dominance is an act, and that there is nothing natural about it. Those who believe in it, therefore, are merely fooling themselves.

Bibliography

PRIMARY SOURCES

Bevington, David ed., *The Complete Works of Shakespeare*, Third Edition. Glenview, IL, 1980. [1]

SECONDARY SOURCES

Baldwin, T. W. *The Organization and Personnel of the Shakespearean Company*. Princeton, 1927. [1]

Berek, Peter. "Text, Gender, and Genre in *The Taming of the Shrew*." In *"Bad" Shakespeare: Revaluations of the Shakespeare Canon*, ed. by Maurice Charney, 91-104. London, 1988. [1]

Boose, Lynda E. "Scolding Brides and Bridling Scolds: Taming the Woman's Unruly Member." *Shakespeare Quarterly* 42 (1991) 179-213. [3]

Fineman, Joel. "The Turn of the Shrew." In *Shakespeare and the Question of Theory*, ed. by Patricia Parker, et al, 138-59. New York, 1985. [4]

Haring-Smith, Tori. *From Farce to Metadrama: A Stage History of "The Taming of the Shrew," 1594-1983* (Contributions in Drama and Theatre Studies, 16). Westport, CT, 1985. [1]

Hodgdon, Barbara. "Katherina Bound; or, Play(K)ating the Strictures of Everyday Life." *Publications of the Modern Language Association of America* 107 (1992) 538-53. [4]

Holderness, Graham. "Production, Reproduction, Performance:

Marxism, History, Theatre." In *Uses of History: Marxism, Postmodernism and the Renaissance*, ed. by Francis Barker, et al, 153-78. Manchester, 1991. [3]

Howard, Jean. "Women as Spectators, Spectacles, and Paying Customers." In *Staging the Renaissance: Reinterpretations of Elizabethan and Jacobean Drama*, ed. by Kastan and Stallybrass, 68-74. New York, 1991. [1] A longer version of this article entitled "Scripts and/versus Playhouses: Ideological Production and the Renaissance Public Stage," appears in *Renaissance Drama* 20 (1989) 31-49. [3]

Howard-Hill, T. H., ed. *The Taming of the Shrew: A Concordance to the Text of the First Folio* (The Oxford Shakespeare Concordances). Oxford, 1969. [1]

Huston, J. Dennis. "'To make a puppet': Play and Play-Making in *The Taming of the Shrew.*" *Shakespeare Studies* 9 (1976) 73-87. [1]

Levine, Laura. "Men in Women's Clothing: Anti-theatricality and Effeminization from 1579 to 1642." *Criticism* 28 (1986) 121-43. [1]

Mikesell, Margaret. "'Love wrought these miracles': Marriage and Genre in *The Taming of the Shrew.*" *Renaissance Drama* 20 (1990) 141-67. [1]

Moison, Thomas. "'Knock me here soundly': Comic Misprision and Class Consciousness in Shakespeare." *Shakespeare Quarterly* 42 (1991) 276-90. See esp. 276-82. [2]

Newman, Karen. "Renaissance Family Politics and Shakespeare's *The Taming of the Shrew.*" *English Literary Renaissance* 16 (1986) 86-100. [3]

Orgell, Stephen. "Nobody's Perfect: Or Why Did the English Stage Take Boys for Women?" *The South Atlantic Quarterly* 88 (1989) 7-29. [1]

Perret, Marion D. "Petruchio: The Model Wife." *Studies in English Literature, 1500-1900* 23 (1983) 223-35. [1]

Sirluck, Katherine A. "Patriarchy, Pedagogy, and the Divided Self in *The Taming of the Shrew.*" *University of Toronto Quarterly* 60 (1990-91) 417-34. [3]

Traub, Valerie. "The (In)significance of 'lesbian' desire in early modern England." In *Erotic Politics: Desire on the Renaissance Stage*, ed. by Susan Zimmerman, 150-69. New York, 1992. [3]

Weller, Barry. "Induction and Inference: Theatre, Transformation, and the Construction of Identity in *The Taming of the Shrew*." In *Creative Imitation: New Essays on Renaissance Literature*, ed. by David Quint, et al, 297-329. Binghamton, 1992. [1]

Wells, Stanley and Gary Taylor. "No Shrew, a Shrew, and the Shrew: Internal Revision in *The Taming of the Shrew*." In *Shakespeare: Text, Language, Criticism*, ed. by Bernhard Fabian, et al, 351-70. New York, 1987. [1]

Wentersdorf, Karl P. "The Original Ending of *The Taming of the Shrew*: A Reconsideration." *Studies in English Literature, 1500-1900* 18 (1978) 201-15. [1]

REA's Test Preps
The Best in Test Preparation

- REA "Test Preps" are far **more** comprehensive than any other test preparation series
- Each book contains up to **eight** full-length practice exams based on the most recent exams
- **Every** type of question likely to be given on the exams is included
- Answers are accompanied by **full** and **detailed** explanations

REA has published over 60 Test Preparation volumes in several series. They include:

Advanced Placement Exams (APs)
Biology
Calculus AB & Calculus BC
Chemistry
Computer Science
English Language & Composition
English Literature & Composition
European History
Government & Politics
Physics
Psychology
Spanish Language
United States History

College Level Examination Program (CLEP)
American History I
Analysis & Interpretation of
  Literature
College Algebra
Freshman College Composition
General Examinations
Human Growth and Development
Introductory Sociology
Principles of Marketing

SAT II: Subject Tests
American History
Biology
Chemistry
French
German
Literature

SAT II: Subject Tests (continued)
Mathematics Level IC, IIC
Physics
Spanish
Writing

Graduate Record Exams (GREs)
Biology
Chemistry
Computer Science
Economics
Engineering
General
History
Literature in English
Mathematics
Physics
Political Science
Psychology
Sociology

ACT - American College Testing
  Assessment

ASVAB - Armed Service Vocational
  Aptitude Battery

CBEST - California Basic Educational
  Skills Test

CDL - Commercial Driver's License Exam

CLAST - College Level Academic Skills
  Test

ELM - Entry Level Mathematics

ExCET - Exam for Certification of
  Educators in Texas

FE (EIT) - Fundamentals of
  Engineering Exam

FE Review - Fundamentals of
  Engineering Review

GED - High School Equivalency
  Diploma Exam (US & Canadian
  editions)

GMAT - Graduate Management
  Admission Test

LSAT - Law School Admission Test

MAT - Miller Analogies Test

MCAT - Medical College Admission
  Test

MSAT - Multiple Subjects
  Assessment for Teachers

NTE - National Teachers Exam

PPST - Pre-Professional Skills Tests

PSAT - Preliminary Scholastic
  Assessment Test

SAT I - Reasoning Test

SAT I - Quick Study & Review

TASP - Texas Academic Skills
  Program

TOEFL - Test of English as a
  Foreign Language

REA's **Problem Solvers**

The "PROBLEM SOLVERS" are comprehensive supplemental text-books designed to save time in finding solutions to problems. Each "PROBLEM SOLVER" is the first of its kind ever produced in its field. It is the product of a massive effort to illustrate almost any imaginable problem in exceptional depth, detail, and clarity. Each problem is worked out in detail with a step-by-step solution, and the problems are arranged in order of complexity from elementary to advanced. Each book is fully indexed for locating problems rapidly.

ACCOUNTING	HEAT TRANSFER
ADVANCED CALCULUS	LINEAR ALGEBRA
ALGEBRA & TRIGONOMETRY	MACHINE DESIGN
AUTOMATIC CONTROL SYSTEMS/ROBOTICS	MATHEMATICS for ENGINEERS
BIOLOGY	MECHANICS
	NUMERICAL ANALYSIS
BUSINESS, ACCOUNTING, & FINANCE	OPERATIONS RESEARCH
CALCULUS	OPTICS
CHEMISTRY	ORGANIC CHEMISTRY
COMPLEX VARIABLES	PHYSICAL CHEMISTRY
COMPUTER SCIENCE	PHYSICS
DIFFERENTIAL EQUATIONS	PRE-CALCULUS
ECONOMICS	PROBABILITY
ELECTRICAL MACHINES	PSYCHOLOGY
ELECTRIC CIRCUITS	STATISTICS
ELECTROMAGNETICS	STRENGTH OF MATERIALS &
ELECTRONIC COMMUNICATIONS	MECHANICS OF SOLIDS
ELECTRONICS	TECHNICAL DESIGN GRAPHICS
FINITE & DISCRETE MATH	THERMODYNAMICS
FLUID MECHANICS/DYNAMICS	TOPOLOGY
GENETICS	TRANSPORT PHENOMENA
GEOMETRY	VECTOR ANALYSIS

*If you would like more information about any of these books,
complete the coupon below and return it to us or visit your local bookstore.*

RESEARCH & EDUCATION ASSOCIATION
61 Ethel Road W. • Piscataway, New Jersey 08854
Phone: (908) 819-8880

Please send me more information about your Problem Solver Books

Name _____

Address _____

City _____ State _____ Zip _____